Hidden Powerful Force at Work

How Micro-Communities Drive Big Change

Must Read Book for all Employees, HR Leaders, DEI Champions, Startup Founders and All Top Management Leaders

5/24/2025

TABLE OF CONTENTS

APPENDIX

Empowering Communities for a Happy Workplace

Book Strategy (ERG/Community Focus)

If you're writing about *Employee Resource Groups or Community Leadership*:

- **Title**: "The Hidden Powerful Force at Work: How Micro-Communities Drive Big Change"
- **Subtitle**: "A guide to launching thriving ERGs for happier, inclusive, and productive workplaces"
- **Target audience**: HR leaders, DEI champions, Startup founders, all Employees and all Top management leaders!
- **Bonus**: Free ERG Launch Checklist, ERG Road map, community templates, or access to a private LinkedIn group

By reading the book *The Hidden Force at Work*, you will:

For HR Leaders & DEI Champions:

- Understand how **Employee Resource Groups (ERGs)** can be a strategic tool for driving inclusion, engagement, and retention.
- Learn how to structure, scale, and measure ERG success using **real-world frameworks, dashboards, and governance models**.
- Gain practical checklists, templates, and launch plans to activate ERGs in your organization—starting immediately.

For Business & People Leaders:

- Discover how **micro-communities transform workplace culture** from the inside out, boosting belonging and business performance.
- Learn how ERGs support talent development, leadership pipelines, and innovation.
- See how emotional connection and community impact productivity, resilience, and loyalty.

For ERG Leaders & Employees:

- Get inspired to **lead or participate in a meaningful ERG**, and build your own leadership skills in the process.
- Explore how ERGs can support **well-being, visibility, personal growth, and happiness** at work.

- Find tools to create events, rally people, sustain engagement, and communicate impact to leadership.

For Startup Founders & Consultants:

- Unlock the power of **communities as cultural architecture**—a key advantage in scaling purpose-driven, people-first companies.
- Position your brand and product as community-aligned by applying principles from ERG strategies.
- Leverage this book as a playbook for designing inclusive, mission-driven organizations.

By the end of this book, you'll walk away with:

- A **deep understanding of how and why ERGs work**
- A **clear roadmap to launch or evolve ERGs**
- Practical tools to **measure ROI and align ERGs with business strategy**
- A compelling vision for a **happier, connected, and more human workplace**

SECTION 1

The Vision behind the Movement

My Calling started here – The Story before this book is born:

Before **After**

My Calling: The Moment This Book Was Born

"To help people feel seen, valued, and happy at work – by empowering community as the hidden force that drives big change."

My Calling: The Moment This Book Was Born

It was a typical Monday morning—8:50 AM. I stepped into the elevator at my office, joining 8 or 9 other colleagues. But something struck me deeply.

No one made eye contact.
No one smiled.
No one even said, "Good morning."

There was an overwhelming sense of isolation, even though we stood just inches apart. The silence was loud. The mood—distant and heavy. It wasn't just "Monday blues"—this felt like something deeper, more chronic, more systemic.

I asked myself:
"Why are we so disconnected?"
"Why does this space feel so joyless?"

At that very moment, something shifted inside me. I knew I couldn't unsee what I had just felt. And I knew this wasn't unique to one office—it was a reflection of what's happening in workplaces around the world.

That moment gave birth to a lifelong purpose:

To build connected, inclusive, and joyful workplaces through the power of communities.

What I Realized:

In most companies, there exists only the formal organizational structure—reporting lines, roles, hierarchies. But what's missing is the **"formal-informal" layer**: authentic, voluntary, people-led **communities** within the workplace. That's where **Employee Resource Groups (ERGs)** come in.

ERGs are **micro-communities** that sit under the formal structure, yet carry the potential to spark real belonging, cross-functional connection, and purpose-driven engagement.

From that elevator ride to this book, my mission has become clear:

"To help people feel seen, valued, and happy at work—by empowering community as the hidden force that drives big change."

My Larger Purpose: Creating a Connected and Belonging World through Communities

I believe I have a larger purpose in life—one that goes beyond career, titles, or roles.

I dream of a world where people are happy, connected, collaborative, and truly belong.
A world, where workplaces are not just productive, but also human.
Where people feel safe, seen, and supported every day.

Let's start with the corporate world. Because today, in many companies:

- Only **24% of employees** report experiencing complete workplace wellbeing (as per global studies).
- Psychological safety is lacking.

- A sense of belonging is missing.
- Disconnection is rising—leading to attrition, disengagement, and unhappiness.

This is not just a "people" issue—it's a **business risk**.
And I believe we have a powerful, often overlooked solution:
ERGs — Employee Resource Groups.

I call ERGs the **"formal-informal layer"** beneath a company's structure.
They are grassroots communities **for employees, by employees** that foster connection, meaning, and inclusion.

ERGs are more than just groups.
They are **micro-communities** that bring:

- Cross-hierarchical connection
- A high sense of belonging
- Safe spaces for diverse voices
- Happiness that fuels innovation and productivity

When people feel they truly belong, they bring their full selves to work.
And when they bring their full selves, companies unlock their **full potential**.

That is the deeper purpose of this book, of UnityCircle, and of my life's work:

To create communities that transform workplaces—and the world—into places of joy, equity, and human connection.

What is an ERG?

An **Employee Resource Group (ERG)** is a **voluntary, employee-led group** within a company that brings together individuals who share a common identity, interest, or life experience — or who support those who do.

Key Characteristics of an ERG

- **Identity or interest-based** (e.g., women, veterans, LGBTQIA+, working parents, book club)
- **Voluntary participation**
- **Employee-led**, but often **executive-sponsored**
- Aims to foster **belonging, inclusion, and engagement**
- Can influence **company policy, culture, and business strategy**

Primary Goals of ERGs

1. **Build Community** – Create a sense of belonging across teams and functions.
2. **Support Inclusion** – Amplify underrepresented voices and drive DEI (Diversity, Equity, Inclusion).
3. **Drive Engagement** – Host events, mentorship programs, and learning opportunities.
4. **Influence Business** – Offer insight into diverse markets and support inclusive practices.
5. **Develop Leaders** – ERG participation helps employees build leadership, project management, and advocacy skills.

- *Women@Google*
- *Black@Facebook*
- *Pride@Salesforce*
- *Veterans@Amazon*
- *Parents@Adobe*

Why ERGs (Communities)?

Why ERGs (Communities) Matter in Workplace

In every organization, there are formal structures—departments, hierarchies, reporting lines. But what's often missing is the **"human infrastructure"** that enables connection, belonging, and joy.

That's where **ERGs—Employee Resource Groups—step in.**

ERGs are **micro-communities** formed by employees, for employees. They are purpose-driven groups built around shared identities, interests, or values—functioning as the *formal-informal* layer beneath the organizational chart.

These communities serve a vital role:
They **bring people together**, break down silos, and create safe spaces for support, learning, and leadership development.

Why We Need Them Now More Than Ever

In today's fast-paced, hybrid, and often isolating work environment:

- Employees feel **disconnected**
- Engagement is dropping
- Belonging is at risk
- Psychological safety is not a given

Yet studies show that when people feel connected and included, **productivity, retention, innovation, and wellbeing soar**.

ERGs Are a Human Solution to a Cultural Problem

ERGs are not "nice to have." They are:

- ☐ **Happiness engines** — bringing joy, connection, and camaraderie
- ☐ **Culture multipliers** — influencing values and behaviors at scale
- ☐ **Innovation accelerators** — offering bottom-up insights and ideas
- ☐ **Leadership incubators** — nurturing talent in safe, empowering spaces

From fitness clubs to book circles, from social justice groups to volunteering squads—ERGs cultivate **a shared sense of purpose**.

They create belonging, and belonging creates momentum.

My Experience

In my own journey—from leading cycling groups in Hyderabad to building workplace communities—I've seen the **transformative power** of micro-communities.

People bond over small joys like morning rides, wellness meetups, or community cleanups. These interactions ripple into trust, collaboration, and shared impact—both inside and outside the workplace.

When employees connect through purpose, they commit with passion.

That's why I believe:

Communities aren't just part of workplace culture—they are the culture.

Why ERGs (Communities) Matter

ERGs are micro-communities formed by employees, for employees.

They bring people together and create support, learning, and leadership development

Why We Need Them Now More Than Ever

- ✓ Disconnected employees
- ✓ Dropping engagement
- ✓ Belonging at risk
- ✓ Psychological safety not a given

ERGs Are a Human Solution to a Cultural Problem

- Happiness engines — bringing joy, connection, and camaraderie
- Culture multipliers — influencing values and behaviors at scale
- Innovation accelerators — offering bottom-up insights and ideas
- Leadership incubators — nurturing talent in safe, empowering spaces

Why ERGs and Micro Communities works, from the lens of Maslow's Hierarchy of Needs

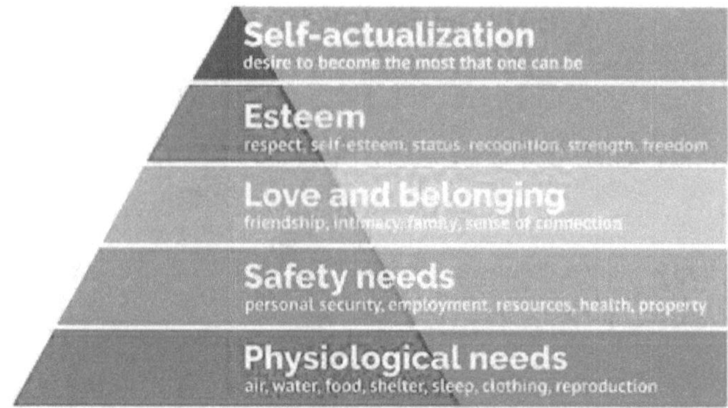

Maslow's hierarchy of needs

Psychological Explanation of Communities

Abraham Maslow's Hierarchy of Needs explains human motivation as a progression through five levels of needs—from survival to self-actualization. When applied to the workplace, this model helps us understand **why ERGs (Employee Resource Groups) and micro-communities are so effective**.

Let's explore each level through this lens:

1. Physiological Needs (Basic Survival)

Food, water, shelter, rest

While these are usually addressed through compensation and physical infrastructure, ERGs can **support access to**

wellness, meals, and resources—especially during crisis or life events. For instance:

- A parenting ERG may organize childcare support.
- A wellness ERG may lead health drives or mental health check-ins.

ERGs amplify how organizations **go beyond policy to meet basic needs with empathy**.

2. Safety Needs

Personal security, financial security, health, stability

ERGs create a **safe psychological space**—especially for marginalized groups. In many companies, employees fear speaking up, expressing identity, or being vulnerable. ERGs counter this by:

- Building **trust-based communities**
- Offering access to **resources, mentorship, and peer support**
- Encouraging a sense of **protection and advocacy**

Belonging starts with **feeling safe**—physically, emotionally, and culturally.

3. Love & Belonging Needs

Friendship, community, connection

This is where ERGs shine brightest.

ERGs foster **inclusive, voluntary spaces** where employees can:

- Form bonds beyond teams and hierarchies
- Participate in group activities, celebrations, or shared causes
- Experience **empathy, laughter, and shared humanity**

When people feel they belong, they thrive. And when they thrive, organizations grow.

---

4. Esteem Needs

Recognition, respect, achievement, status

ERGs empower members to take initiative, lead events, and drive change—giving them:

- **Visibility** beyond their roles
- **Leadership development opportunities**
- **Appreciation and recognition** from peers and leaders

ERGs create leaders from every level—not just the top.

---

5. Self-Actualization

Growth, purpose, creativity, becoming your best self

At the highest level, ERGs help employees **find meaning** in their work. People begin to see their workplace as a **platform for purpose**, not just a job.

Whether they lead an LGBTQ+ ERG, run a cultural celebration, or drive sustainability efforts, members feel:

- **Aligned with their values**
- **Part of something bigger**
- **Proud of who they are and what they do**

ERGs unlock human potential by giving employees a voice, a mission, and a community.

Final Thought:

Maslow's hierarchy reminds us that to unleash true performance, **we must meet human needs at every level**—not just provide salaries and goals.
ERGs and micro-communities are the hidden engines that do exactly that.

They don't just make companies better.

They make people feel whole.

Scientific Explanation of Communities

The Scientific Explanation of Why Communities Matter

While communities are often seen as social or emotional constructs, their impact is also deeply **scientific**. Human beings are biologically wired for connection. The sense of belonging we experience in communities—especially in Employee Resource Groups (ERGs)—isn't just a "nice to have." It directly affects our **brain chemistry, emotional wellbeing, and performance**.

Let's explore the science behind this:

The Brain on Belonging: The Chemistry of Connection

When we engage in meaningful community interactions—whether a coffee chat, cycling group, or ERG session—our brain releases a powerful mix of neurotransmitters and hormones that drive **trust, happiness, and bonding**.

Dopamine – The reward hormone

Triggered by goal completion, appreciation, or small wins within communities.
Example: Organizing a successful ERG event or helping a teammate

Oxytocin – The bonding hormone

Increases through trust, emotional sharing, and group affiliation.
Example: Feeling connected during team discussions, rituals, or ERG storytelling circles

Serotonin – The pride & wellbeing hormone

Released when we feel respected, included, and valued by peers.
Example: Receiving recognition or being invited to lead within a community

Endorphins – The feel-good stress reducers

Elevated during laughter, exercise, or shared celebrations.
Example: Community outings, wellness sessions, or joyful moments within ERGs

Conclusion: Communities are not just social spaces—they are **neural networks of happiness and trust**.

The Biological Need for Belonging

Psychologists like Roy Baumeister and Abraham Maslow have emphasized that **belonging is a fundamental human need**, as vital as food or safety. Chronic loneliness and disconnection, in contrast, have been linked to:

- Increased cortisol (stress hormone)
- Lower immunity
- Reduced motivation and cognitive performance

When employees feel isolated at work, their body registers it as a **threat state**—impacting focus, trust, and engagement. Communities counter this by activating the **"safe zone" in the brain**.

The Business-Science Bridge

Workplace communities—especially ERGs—bridge the gap between **emotional wellbeing and organizational performance**. They:

- Lower stress and burnout
- Increase psychological safety
- Enhance learning and collaboration
- Create space for authenticity and creativity

Neuroscience confirms what we instinctively know: **When people feel connected, they perform better, stay longer, and thrive deeper.**

SECTION 2

Understanding ERGs
The Heart of Modern Workplace

Different Types of ERG

ERG - Employee Resource Groups are small groups lead by Employees, for Employees.

Employee Resource Groups (ERGs) typically form around shared identities, experiences, or interests. Here are the most common **types of ERGs**, categorized by theme:

⬜ Identity-Based ERGs

These focus on shared demographic or cultural identity:

- **Gender-based**:
  - Women in the Workplace
  - Men as Allies
  - Non-binary & Gender Nonconforming Support
- **Race & Ethnicity**:
  - Black/African American
  - Latinx/Hispanic
  - Asian & Pacific Islander
  - Indigenous Peoples
- **LGBTQIA+**:
  - Pride Network
  - Queer Allies
  - Trans & Non-Binary Advocacy
- **Generational**:
  - Millennials/Gen Z
  - Gen X & Boomers
  - Multigenerational Collaboration
- **Disability & Neurodiversity**:
  - Disability Inclusion
  - Mental Health & Wellness

- o Neurodiverse Talent
- **Veterans & Military Families**:
  - o Veterans Support
  - o Military Spouse Network
- **Religion & Faith**:
  - o Interfaith Network
  - o Faith-Specific Groups (Christian, Muslim, Hindu, Jewish, etc.)

▢ Interest- or Role-Based ERGs

These foster connections across departments or shared passions:

- **Working Parents & Caregivers**
- **Remote & Hybrid Workers**
- **Young Professionals / Early Career**
- **Sustainability & Green Teams**
- **Tech Women / Women in STEM**
- **First-Generation Professionals**

Affinity + Allyship ERGs

Some ERGs explicitly include **allies** in the name to encourage broader participation:

- e.g., *Black & Allies Network, Women+, LGBTQIA+ & Allies*

Hobbies-based ERGs (also called *interest-based* or *passion-based groups*) are centered around shared activities, passions, or lifestyle interests rather than identity or professional role. These groups foster **cross-functional connection, employee engagement**, and **well-being**.

⬜ Common Categories of Hobby-Based ERGs

Sports & Fitness

- Running Club / Marathoners
- Cycling Group (like your own work with cycling!)
- Yoga & Mindfulness
- Hiking & Outdoor Adventures
- Company Sports Teams (Cricket, Soccer, Basketball)

Gaming & Technology

- Board Games & Tabletop
- Video Game Guild / eSports Team
- Coding for Fun / Hackathons
- Tech Gadgets & Innovation

Arts & Culture

- Book Club
- Film Appreciation / Movie Buffs
- Photography Enthusiasts
- Performing Arts (Music, Dance, Drama)
- Visual Arts Collective (Painting, Sketching)

Lifestyle & Wellness

- Gardening & Urban Farming
- Foodies & Culinary ERG (Cooking, Baking, Tasting Events)
- Sustainability & Green Living
- Mindfulness & Meditation

Social Impact & Volunteering

- Community Outreach / Giving Back
- Environmental Action Group
- Education & Mentorship Volunteers

Travel & Language

- World Travelers Network
- Language Exchange & Multilingual Clubs
- Cultural Exchange & Heritage Travel

Why Hobbies-Based ERGs Matter

- Encourage **cross-team bonding** beyond work roles
- Improve **mental wellness** and reduce burnout
- Support **creative expression** and **authentic connections**
- Increase **participation** from employees who may not identify with traditional affinity groups

Top 25 Examples of ERGs in Companies Today 2025

Employee Resource Groups (ERGs) are critical for fostering diversity, inclusion, and a sense of belonging within organizations. They provide employees with support, professional development, and a platform to contribute to their community's mission. Below are 25 top example ERGs in companies, showcasing how they can address various aspects of inclusion:

1. Google - Women@Google

- **Focus**: Empowering women in tech, advocating for gender equality, and creating a network for mentorship and professional development.

2. Microsoft - Blacks at Microsoft (BAM)

- **Focus**: Supporting Black employees through mentorship, community outreach, and initiatives aimed at increasing diversity in the tech industry.

3. Salesforce - Ohana

- **Focus**: Salesforce's overarching ERG supporting diverse groups including LGBTQ+, people of color, women, and veterans, emphasizing the company's family-like culture.

4. Intel - Intel's Women's Leadership Council

- **Focus**: Promoting gender diversity, creating leadership opportunities, and offering networking and development programs for women in tech.

5. IBM - Black and African American Network

- **Focus**: Empowering Black employees by offering professional development, leadership programs, and providing a platform for advocacy within the company.

6. Citi - Women's Network

- **Focus**: Advancing gender equality in financial services, promoting women's leadership, and creating mentorship opportunities for women at Citi.

7. Facebook - Facebook Women@

- **Focus**: Creating a network for women at Facebook, supporting professional growth, and advancing leadership opportunities for women in tech and business.

8. Accenture - LGBTQ+ ERG

- **Focus**: Promoting inclusion for the LGBTQ+ community, offering support and advocacy, and working to ensure equitable treatment across the company.

9. PepsiCo - Women's Inclusion Network (WIN)

- **Focus**: Advocating for gender equality, increasing women's representation in leadership, and providing networking and professional development for women.

10. Johnson & Johnson - J&J PRIDE

- **Focus**: Supporting LGBTQ+ employees by advocating for equal rights and providing a community for personal and professional growth.

11. American Express - Women in Technology

- **Focus**: Empowering women in technology roles, providing mentorship, and fostering a diverse pipeline for women in leadership positions.

12. Dell Technologies - Multicultural ERG

- **Focus**: Supporting employees of diverse cultural backgrounds, promoting inclusivity, and advancing opportunities for minorities within the company.

13. SAP - Autism at Work

- **Focus**: Promoting inclusion for employees with autism, offering mentorship and job coaching, and building a more neurodiverse workforce.

14. Coca-Cola - Coca-Cola Women's Leadership Council

- **Focus**: Supporting the advancement of women in leadership roles at Coca-Cola through mentorship, professional development, and community outreach programs.

15. Verizon - Verizon Pride

- **Focus**: Providing a supportive space for LGBTQ+ employees, advocating for equality, and celebrating diversity through events and initiatives.

16. Nike - Black Employee Network

- **Focus**: Supporting Black employees by providing networking opportunities, mentorship, and advocating for increased representation in leadership roles.

17. LinkedIn - LinkedIn for Women

- **Focus**: Empowering women through mentorship, professional development, and creating a platform for discussing gender equality in the workplace.

18. Wells Fargo - Women's Team Member Network

- **Focus**: Providing networking and leadership opportunities for women, focusing on career development and creating a more inclusive environment for women at Wells Fargo.

19. Twitter - Twitter Women@

- **Focus**: Advocating for women's leadership, offering networking and mentorship programs, and creating a space for women to discuss challenges and opportunities in tech.

20. Uber - Uber Pride

- **Focus**: Supporting and advocating for the LGBTQ+ community, creating a safe space for LGBTQ+ employees, and celebrating Pride month through company-wide initiatives.

21. Uber - Black@Uber

- **Focus**: Empowering Black employees at Uber through mentorship, community support, and offering programs for professional development and leadership growth.

22. Adobe - Adobe Pride

- **Focus**: Advocating for LGBTQ+ rights, fostering inclusivity, and supporting LGBTQ+ employees through networking and resources for professional development.

23. Airbnb - Airbnb Pride

- **Focus**: Supporting LGBTQ+ employees by creating a safe and inclusive environment, hosting events, and advocating for equal rights within the company and beyond.

24. Netflix - Black @ Netflix

- **Focus**: Supporting Black employees, increasing representation in leadership, and fostering a strong sense of community for Black employees within the company.

25. Bain & Company - Women@Bain

- **Focus**: Empowering women in consulting, providing mentorship, and promoting leadership opportunities for women in the business consulting industry.

These ERGs show the diversity of focus areas, from gender and racial inclusivity to supporting neurodiversity and LGBTQ+ employees. The key to their success is creating a safe space where employees feel supported, valued, and heard, and where they can access opportunities for growth and leadership. Companies that embrace ERGs contribute not only to the professional development of individuals but also to the broader goal of creating a more inclusive workplace culture.

Understanding the Evolution and Impact of Employee Communities

In today's evolving workplaces, employee-led communities have become vital for fostering connection, inclusion, and engagement. But as these groups mature, many companies face a common question: **What's the difference between an affinity group and an Employee Resource Group (ERG)?** And when should one evolve into the other?

In this article, we explore the transition **from affinity groups to ERGs**, unpack the distinction between the two, and explain how formalizing employee communities can drive deeper organizational impact.

ERG vs Affinity Group: What's the Difference?

At first glance, **affinity groups** and **ERGs** might seem interchangeable—they both bring together employees with shared identities or interests. However, there are key differences in structure, purpose, and strategic alignment.

Feature	Affinity Group	Employee Resource Group (ERG)
Formality	Informal, grassroots	Structured and often recognized by HR or leadership
Goals	Build community, offer peer support	Drive business impact, inclusion, and engagement goals
Sponsorship	May or may not have executive support	Typically has executive sponsor or leadership liaison
Funding	Rarely funded	Usually receives budget and resources
Accountability	Operates independently	Aligned with DEI strategy and measured for impact

Why Companies Transition from Affinity Groups to ERGs

As organizations mature in their DEI journeys, many affinity groups evolve into ERGs for several reasons:

1. Increased Strategic Value

ERGs can tie their activities to broader business outcomes—such as improving recruitment, retention, or product inclusion. This helps the organization see these groups as essential to company success, not just social clubs.

2. Access to Resources

Formal recognition brings support. ERGs often receive:

- Budget for events, training, and speakers
- Access to internal communication platforms
- Inclusion in organizational planning and decision-making

3. Greater Visibility and Influence

With executive sponsorship and measurable goals, ERGs gain a seat at the table. Their input can influence hiring practices, policies, and even customer-facing strategies.

4. Leadership Development

ERGs offer leadership roles and project experience for underrepresented talent, building a pipeline of future leaders.

How to Evolve from an Affinity Group to an ERG

Ready to make the transition? Here are the steps:

1. **Define Your Mission & Goals** Align the group's purpose with both community needs and business objectives.
2. **Secure Executive Sponsorship** Partner with a leader who can advocate for the group and help navigate internal processes.
3. **Develop a Governance Structure** Establish roles (chair, treasurer, communications lead), decision-making norms, and regular meeting cadences.

4. **Request Budget and Resources** Work with HR or DEI teams to allocate funding for events, software, or professional development.
5. **Start Measuring Impact** Track engagement, event participation, and influence on retention or culture to demonstrate ROI.

UnityCircle: Supporting the Evolution of Employee Communities

Whether you're starting with grassroots affinity groups or scaling a formal ERG strategy, **UnityCircle** helps organizations:

- Centralize communication and event management
- Track membership and engagement data
- Provide ERG leaders with tools and templates
- Align ERG work with company-wide DEI goals

Ready to take your employee groups to the next level? Explore UnityCircle and see how we support every stage of the journey from affinity to impact.

Final Thoughts

The shift **from affinity groups to ERGs** represents more than just formalization—it's a signal that a company values diversity, voices, and belonging at every level. By elevating these communities, organizations don't just support their employees—they empower them to lead change.

Because when employees lead, companies grow stronger.

SECTION 3

Benefits of ERGs for Employees and Organizations

Benefits of ERGs

Benefits for Employees

Sense of Belonging

- Safe space to connect with others who share similar identities, experiences, or interests.

Community & Support

- Emotional support, mentorship, and camaraderie across departments and job levels.

Professional Development

- Leadership opportunities, public speaking, event planning, and networking.

Voice & Visibility

- A platform to share concerns, ideas, and experiences with leadership.

Cultural Awareness

- Exposure to different perspectives and communities, even as an ally.

Benefits for Organizations

Employee Engagement & Retention

- o Employees who feel seen and supported are more likely to stay and perform better.

Leadership Pipeline

- o ERG leaders often emerge as high-potential talent with cross-functional experience.

Diversity, Equity & Inclusion (DEI) Impact

- o ERGs can guide inclusive policies, practices, and recruiting strategies.

Business Insights

- o ERGs help companies understand diverse markets and customer needs (e.g., product feedback, localization).

Positive Employer Brand

- o Public support for ERGs enhances reputation with candidates and consumers alike.

Crisis & Change Support

- o ERGs often play a key role in helping companies navigate social issues or internal culture shifts.

ERGs and Business Outcomes Benefits Matrix

ERG Benefits Matrix: Activities vs. Business Outcomes

ERG Activity	Employee Outcome	Business Impact
Hosting cultural events & celebrations	Sense of belonging, inclusion	Improved engagement, reduced turnover
Peer mentoring & coaching	Career growth, confidence	Leadership pipeline development
Storytelling & panel discussions	Employee voice, visibility	DEI culture and brand enhancement
Organizing volunteer activities	Purpose, team bonding	Community goodwill, ESG reporting support
Allyship training & workshops	Awareness, behavioral change	Inclusive culture, lower bias-driven attrition
Feedback to HR/leadership	Empowerment, trust	Informed DEI strategy, better talent policies
Networking events across ERGs	Cross-team relationships, exposure	Stronger collaboration, idea sharing
Surveying ERG members	Data-driven improvements	Insight into employee needs and engagement drivers
Product or service input (e.g. for diverse markets)	Influence, value recognition	Better market fit, customer experience innovation

Factors of Happiness for Employees at workplace?

Employee happiness at the workplace is driven by a mix of **emotional, social, environmental, and professional factors**. When these are in balance, people feel fulfilled, motivated, and committed to their work and workplace.

⬛ Key Factors That Drive Employee Happiness

1. Belonging & Inclusion

- Feeling **accepted, respected, and included** as oneself
- Having strong social connections with colleagues
- Being part of inclusive ERGs or communities

2. Purpose & Meaning

- Understanding how one's work **matters**
- Feeling aligned with the company's **mission and values**
- Opportunities to contribute to something **bigger than a job**

3. Growth & Development

- Access to **learning, upskilling, and mentorship**
- Clear career pathways and **internal mobility**
- Stretch assignments and leadership roles (e.g., in ERGs)

4. Psychological Safety

- Confidence to speak up without fear of judgment

- Trust in leadership and fair decision-making
- Support for mental well-being

5. Recognition & Feedback

- Being appreciated for effort and contributions
- Frequent, meaningful feedback — not just annual reviews
- Peer-to-peer recognition platforms and rituals

6. Work-Life Balance

- Flexibility in when, where, and how work gets done
- Support for parents, caregivers, and wellness needs
- Reasonable workloads and expectations

7. Fair Compensation & Benefits

- Competitive salary and benefits
- Perks that reflect employee needs (health, financial wellness, flexibility)

8. Positive Work Environment

- Safe, clean, and inspiring physical (or digital) workspaces
- Opportunities for social interaction and team building
- A culture of respect, empathy, and collaboration

UnityCircle Tie-In

Many of these factors — **belonging, purpose, recognition, development, and inclusion** — are directly supported through **strong ERGs and community culture**, which UnityCircle enables.

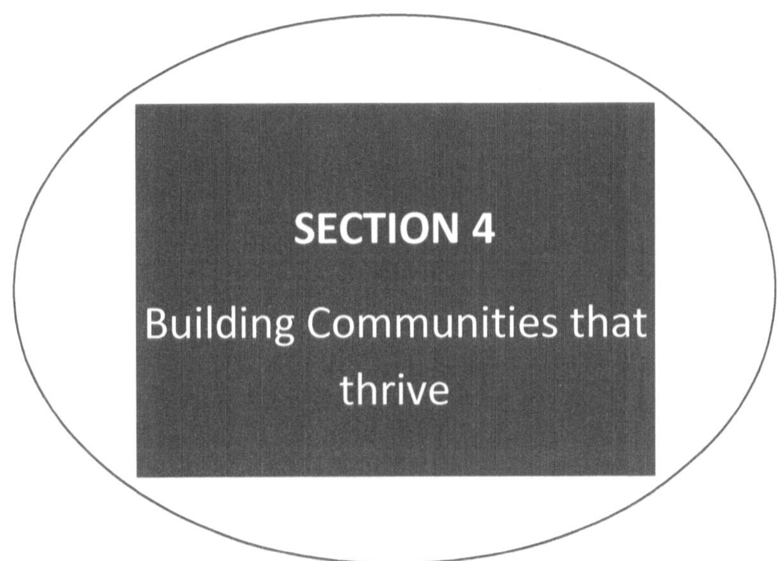

SECTION 4

Building Communities that thrive

How ERGs (Communities) are born?

The Community Leader has to be passionate about the topic or area, for which he/she is forming the community for. There has to be purpose to the community. There has to be a problem statement to the ERG. Better to use the ERG checklist and ERG charter for creation and launching one. On top of this, there has to be a need for it either identified by the leader or the community members feel for it.

Why Communities Are Needed

Communities are needed because they fulfill deep human, social, and organizational needs that go **beyond transactions and structures** — they provide **connection, identity, support, and collective strength**.

Why Communities Are Needed

1. Human Connection & Belonging

- People **thrive in groups** where they are seen, heard, and valued.
- Communities **combat isolation**, especially in remote or hybrid work environments.
- Belonging improves **mental health, retention, and performance**.

2. Shared Learning & Growth

- Communities foster **peer-to-peer learning**, mentoring, and skill sharing.
- Collective wisdom emerges faster than top-down knowledge systems.

- They create **safe environments** to ask questions and experiment.

3. Engagement & Motivation

- A strong community boosts **intrinsic motivation** through purpose and recognition.
- Rituals, traditions, and shared goals increase **participation and loyalty**.
- People give more when they feel like they **matter to others**.

4. Voice, Visibility & Advocacy

- Communities provide a **platform for underrepresented voices** to be heard.
- They become **vehicles for advocacy, culture change, and innovation**.
- ERGs are a great example—employees shaping policy and experience.

5. Meaning & Identity

- People find meaning through **shared values, purpose, and cultural expression**.
- Communities help individuals understand who they are in the context of a group.

6. Business Impact

- In companies, communities drive **collaboration, retention, innovation**, and **employee-led transformation**.
- External communities (e.g., customers, partners) build **brand loyalty** and **market intelligence**.

Communities are the **engine** of your platform:

- ERGs **are** communities.
- Your software provides the **infrastructure** for them to **form, grow, and lead**.
- UnityCircle exists because companies need a **system to build community intentionally**.

Invisible Connections lead to Unbreakable Bonds

Invisible connections are often the foundation of strong, resilient communities. These connections, though not always apparent on the surface, form the emotional and social fabric that holds a community together. They are built on shared experiences, mutual understanding, and a deep sense of belonging. Over time, these invisible threads strengthen, transforming into unbreakable bonds that create a sense of unity and purpose. Here's how that process happens:

1. Shared Experiences Create Emotional Bonds

- **The power of shared history:** Communities often begin with shared experiences—whether it's overcoming a challenge, celebrating a success, or navigating a period of change. These moments create emotional resonance, forming connections between individuals that transcend mere interaction.
- **Rituals and traditions:** Regular communal activities, whether formal or informal, like annual events, gatherings, or even everyday interactions, build emotional memories. These shared rituals, even though they may seem trivial, solidify bonds by evoking a sense of nostalgia and belonging.
- **Collective triumphs and struggles:** Whether it's a victory or a setback, going through something together creates a powerful emotional tie. These experiences become a part of the community's shared narrative and reinforce the invisible connections that unite individuals.

2. Mutual Support Strengthens Trust

- **Caring for one another:** In thriving communities, members look out for each other, offering help in times of need and celebrating one another's achievements. This mutual care fosters trust, which is the cornerstone of any strong community.
- **Emotional investment in each other:** The more individuals invest emotionally in one another, the deeper the bond becomes. These invisible connections become unbreakable as people feel valued, understood, and appreciated by their community members.
- **Empathy and understanding:** Communities thrive when individuals empathize with each other's challenges and joys. This emotional intelligence creates deep, invisible threads that bind people together. When people know that others genuinely understand them, the sense of trust grows stronger, making those bonds harder to sever.

3. Inclusive Culture Fosters a Sense of Belonging

- **Creating spaces for everyone:** In an inclusive community, individuals from diverse backgrounds, perspectives, and experiences find common ground. This inclusivity creates invisible connections as people start to see themselves as part of something larger than themselves.
- **Shared values and mission:** A community with a clear set of shared values or a collective mission gives people something to emotionally invest in. These values serve as the invisible glue that holds the group together, even when external circumstances change or challenges arise.

- **Celebrating individuality within the collective:** When communities honor the unique contributions of each individual, they reinforce the emotional bonds between members. People feel seen and appreciated for who they are, not just for what they do.

4. Communication as the Thread That Weaves

- **Frequent, authentic communication:** Open, honest, and vulnerable communication is key to maintaining and strengthening invisible connections. When people feel they can express themselves openly, they form a deeper connection with the community.
- **Non-verbal cues and emotional resonance:** Often, bonds are formed not just through words, but through actions, gestures, and shared silences. These non-verbal cues, whether it's a reassuring look or a helping hand, are powerful indicators of emotional connection.
- **Storytelling:** Sharing stories, whether about personal journeys, struggles, or successes, helps to create emotional connections. These stories create shared understanding and a sense of camaraderie that binds people together, even if they don't interact regularly.

5. Leadership and Emotional Intelligence

- **Leaders who model connection:** Leaders who demonstrate emotional intelligence, empathy, and care for their community's well-being set the tone for the whole group. When leaders actively nurture invisible connections, they inspire others to do the same.

- **Guiding through empathy:** In challenging times, leaders who approach problems with empathy rather than authority help strengthen bonds. Emotional leadership creates trust, making the invisible connections between community members even stronger.

6. Resilience Through Collective Identity

- **Shared sense of purpose:** Communities with a strong collective identity can weather challenges better because the bonds between individuals are rooted in shared purpose. This collective identity, rooted in emotional connections, is the foundation of resilience.
- **Emotional resilience:** The invisible connections formed in a community help individuals cope with stress and adversity. Knowing that others care and are there for them makes the emotional bonds unbreakable, as people know they won't have to face hardship alone.

7. Creating a Legacy of Connection

- **Passing down emotional wisdom:** Over time, communities develop a kind of emotional wisdom that gets passed from one generation or group of individuals to the next. These lessons, learned through shared experiences, create deep emotional ties that are hard to sever.
- **Generational bonds:** As members pass on traditions, rituals, and stories, the invisible connections are strengthened across generations. This creates a sense of continuity and shared legacy, further solidifying the unbreakable nature of the bonds.

In summary, invisible connections become unbreakable bonds in communities through shared experiences, mutual support, inclusive culture, communication, and emotional leadership. These connections are nurtured over time, gradually growing into an unshakeable network of trust, empathy, and belonging. As people invest in each other emotionally, these bonds transform into something that can weather any storm, ensuring that the community remains strong and united.

Building Communities Brick by Brick

Building a community "brick by brick" means carefully constructing a strong foundation, fostering trust, and nurturing relationships one step at a time. Much like constructing a physical building, building a community requires thoughtful planning, effort, and consistent commitment. Here's a step-by-step guide on how to build a community that stands the test of time:

1. Start with a Strong Purpose

- **Define the "why":** Every great community starts with a clear, compelling purpose. Why does your community exist? What need does it fulfill? Whether it's to support a specific group, share knowledge, foster a sense of belonging, or drive a cause, the purpose should be the first "brick" in your community's foundation.
- **Mission and values:** Establish the core values that will guide your community. These values will serve as a compass for decision-making and help maintain focus as the community grows.

2. Identify and Connect with Like-Minded Individuals

- **Seek out early supporters:** Start by identifying people who align with your purpose and values. These early members should be passionate and invested in the mission. They will help set the tone and culture of the community.
- **Foster early connections:** Build relationships with these initial members through personal engagement. Whether it's one-on-one conversations, small meetups, or virtual introductions, these relationships are the first bonds that hold the community together.

3. Create a Welcoming and Inclusive Environment

- **Ensure everyone feels valued:** A community should be a space where everyone feels welcomed and respected. Focus on building an inclusive culture where diversity of thought, background, and experience is not just accepted but celebrated.
- **Encourage participation:** Early on, ensure there are opportunities for people to contribute in meaningful ways. Whether through sharing ideas, participating in discussions, or contributing to community-building activities, make sure every member has a role to play.

4. Establish Communication Channels

- **Choose the right platform:** Find a communication platform that works for your community—whether it's a social media group, a forum, a Slack channel, or regular in-person

events. The key is to ensure it's accessible, user-friendly, and where people can engage easily.
- **Consistent communication:** Regular, clear communication is vital. Keep the community informed about important updates, activities, and progress. Consistency helps build trust and keeps members engaged.

5. Encourage Meaningful Engagement

- **Create value for members:** Offer content, resources, or experiences that are valuable to your members. This could be in the form of exclusive events, educational opportunities, or access to networks that help them grow personally or professionally.
- **Facilitate interaction:** Design activities that encourage members to connect with each other. Whether through collaborative projects, discussion forums, or virtual hangouts, fostering interactions helps build relationships that are the glue of the community.

6. Nurture Leadership and Empower Others

- **Empower community leaders:** As the community grows, it's important to identify and cultivate leaders within the group. These individuals can take on roles that help manage activities, facilitate discussions, and maintain the community's values. Encourage them to take initiative and act as stewards for the community's culture.
- **Delegate responsibilities:** Empower members by giving them opportunities to lead initiatives, contribute to content, or help organize events. This not only eases your workload but also gives

members a sense of ownership and commitment to the community's success.

7. Create Rituals and Traditions

- **Establish shared experiences:** Whether it's an annual event, a regular meeting, or a unique tradition, creating moments that members can look forward to strengthens the emotional bonds within the community.
- **Celebrate milestones:** Acknowledge significant moments, such as reaching community milestones, personal achievements, or the completion of projects. These celebrations help reinforce the sense of collective success and belonging.

8. Foster Trust and Transparency

- **Be open and transparent:** Trust is built over time, and transparency is key. Be honest about the community's goals, challenges, and achievements. When members feel they can trust the leadership and the community as a whole, they're more likely to invest emotionally.
- **Handle conflicts with care:** Conflicts are inevitable, but how they're handled matters. Address issues respectfully, listen to all sides, and strive for solutions that maintain harmony within the group. By handling disputes constructively, you reinforce trust.

9. Adapt and Evolve

- **Stay flexible:** Communities evolve over time, and it's important to be adaptable to change. Regularly assess what's working and what isn't. Solicit feedback from members and be open to adjustments that can improve the community experience.

- **Innovate and grow:** As the community grows, find ways to innovate and keep it fresh. This might include introducing new activities, launching subgroups based on specific interests, or leveraging new technologies to improve engagement.

10. Strengthen Bonds Through Emotional Support

- **Provide a supportive environment:** Ensure that your community is not just about transactional interactions but emotional connection. A community that supports its members during difficult times, celebrates personal milestones, and offers encouragement will have stronger and more lasting bonds.
- **Foster empathy:** Encourage members to support one another, listen actively, and share in each other's challenges and successes. The emotional support people provide to one another is a critical component of building unbreakable community bonds.

11. Celebrate and Reflect

- **Acknowledge progress:** Take time to reflect on how far the community has come. Celebrate achievements, whether it's the growth of membership, a successful initiative, or the deepening of connections. Recognizing the journey strengthens the bonds and gives members a sense of pride in being part of the community.
- **Continue to build on the foundation:** Each brick you lay in the community's foundation—each

connection, conversation, and shared experience—
should be built on the next. Keep adding to the
foundation as your community grows and evolves,
ensuring that each new member feels like a part of
the structure.

In conclusion, building a community brick by brick
requires time, patience, and intentional effort. By focusing
on purpose, inclusivity, communication, and meaningful
engagement, you create a strong and resilient community
that grows organically. Every interaction, every piece of
shared value, and every connection between members
adds to the solid foundation, eventually resulting in a
thriving, unbreakable community.

Emotional Architecture of Community

"The Emotional Architecture of Community" is a
powerful concept that touches on the ways emotions
shape and drive the dynamics of communities. It's the
invisible yet vital force that builds the foundation of trust,
connection, and a sense of belonging. Here's an
exploration of what it could encompass:

1. Emotional Safety and Vulnerability

- **Trust as a cornerstone:** For a community to
  thrive, there needs to be a sense of emotional
  safety. This means creating spaces where
  individuals feel comfortable being vulnerable,
  sharing their authentic selves without fear of
  judgment or ridicule.

- **Safe spaces for expression:** Communities need to offer environments where people can express emotions openly, from joy to grief, and feel heard and supported.

2. Shared Purpose and Collective Identity

- **Creating a unified emotional vision:** Communities often rally around a common goal or purpose. This shared emotional investment creates a collective identity. It's not just about shared activities, but shared emotional experiences—celebrating wins together, mourning losses, and enduring challenges as one.
- **Storytelling as emotional glue:** Stories within a community often bind people together. They allow individuals to relate to one another's struggles, joys, and growth, contributing to a shared emotional journey.

3. Belonging and Inclusion

- **Emotional connection over time:** The sense of belonging is powerful—people want to feel part of something bigger than themselves. Emotional architecture provides the framework for this belonging, ensuring that inclusion isn't just a surface-level effort but a deep, emotional experience.
- **Cultural resonance:** The values, traditions, and rituals of a community serve as emotional touchstones. When they resonate with people's deeper desires and needs, they create bonds that go beyond transactional interactions.

4. Emotional Intelligence in Leadership

- **Empathetic leadership:** Leaders within a community, whether formal or informal, play a pivotal role in managing the emotional landscape. Leaders who practice emotional intelligence, who can sense and respond to the emotional needs of the community, help maintain cohesion and guide the community through emotional highs and lows.
- **Conflict resolution with empathy:** In any group, conflict is inevitable. The ability to manage and resolve conflicts in a way that respects emotions, values, and perspectives fosters a healthy community dynamic.

5. Emotional Rituals and Symbols

- **Creating emotional landmarks:** Communities often have rituals, traditions, or symbols that evoke strong emotional responses. These can be annual events, celebrations, or even symbols like logos or phrases that reinforce the community's identity and emotional ties.
- **Emotional rhythm through regular interactions:** Just as architecture creates physical space, the emotional architecture of community is structured through regular, meaningful interactions—meetings, events, check-ins, etc. These emotional rhythms build familiarity and connection over time.

6. Resilience and Healing

- **Rising through adversity:** Communities are often defined by their ability to navigate adversity together. Emotional resilience is built through

collective experiences of overcoming challenges,
offering mutual support, and healing.

- **Collective emotional intelligence:** A community
that is emotionally intelligent can identify and
process shared pain or joy, helping it to recover
from difficult times and celebrate its successes.

7. Emotional Sustainability

- **Preventing burnout:** Communities need
emotional sustainability—ensuring that the
emotional investments people make in the
community don't lead to exhaustion or burnout.
This requires creating space for people to
recharge, ensuring there's a balance between
emotional input and personal care.
- **Sustaining motivation:** Just as a physical
structure requires maintenance, emotional
architecture needs continuous nurturing.
Communities should actively engage with the
emotional needs of members, ensuring that the
emotional tone is positive, inclusive, and forward-
moving.

In summary, the emotional architecture of a community is
as integral as its physical or structural framework. It
requires careful attention to emotional safety, shared
purpose, empathetic leadership, and rituals that foster
connection. This invisible but potent framework helps
ensure that communities are not just spaces for
interaction, but deeply connected ecosystems where
people feel truly seen, heard, and valued.

Visioning a Connected Future

"Visioning a Connected Future" is an inspiring and forward-looking concept, one that emphasizes the importance of interconnectedness in building a better tomorrow. It's about imagining how individuals, organizations, and communities can come together, bridging gaps, and leveraging technology, empathy, and shared purpose to create a world where collaboration, understanding, and shared growth are at the heart of societal progress. Here's how we can approach visioning a connected future:

1. Building Inclusive and Equitable Connections

- **Access for all:** A connected future means ensuring that everyone has equal access to resources, opportunities, and networks. Whether it's through technology, education, or economic opportunities, an equitable connection across society ensures that no one is left behind.
- **Embracing diversity:** In a connected world, diversity—whether cultural, social, or professional—should be celebrated. Communities should strive for inclusivity, where people from all walks of life feel valued and have an equal chance to contribute and succeed.

2. Fostering Global Collaboration

- **Transcending borders:** A connected future envisions a world where geographic and cultural boundaries become less significant in the way we collaborate. With global collaboration tools,

remote working, and digital communities, people
from different countries and backgrounds can
contribute to common goals in real-time.

- **Shared global challenges:** Whether it's
addressing climate change, economic inequality,
or global health crises, the vision of a connected
future includes united global efforts where
communities and organizations come together to
solve problems that affect us all.

3. Leveraging Technology for Positive Impact

- **Technological empowerment:** Technology
should be used to connect people, facilitate
collaboration, and empower individuals. This
means improving access to knowledge, advancing
digital literacy, and ensuring that technology
serves humanity's collective good rather than
deepening divisions.
- **Smart cities and sustainability:** A connected
future means leveraging technology to build
smarter cities—where infrastructure, resources,
and information are optimized to create more
sustainable and efficient environments for people.
It also includes innovations in renewable energy,
waste management, and eco-friendly practices that
help conserve the planet.

4. Building Emotional and Social Connections

- **Humanizing technology:** While technology can
connect us in unprecedented ways, it's important
to remember the human element. A connected
future should not be solely based on technology; it
should foster emotional, social, and meaningful
relationships. Encouraging empathy, trust, and
genuine human interaction is key to building a

future that balances digital progress with emotional well-being.
- **Social networks as support systems:** Social media and digital platforms should evolve to not just provide entertainment or information, but to create support systems—places where people can connect with others who share similar values or experiences. Whether through peer support groups, mentorship networks, or advocacy platforms, these networks can serve as a safe space for connection and mutual care.

5. Creating Collaborative Communities

- **Community-driven innovation:** A connected future involves the rise of collaborative communities where innovation and progress come from the collective efforts of individuals working together. These communities could be built around shared goals, such as solving local issues, enhancing education, or advancing creative arts. Each member contributes their skills and resources, leading to creative, shared solutions.
- **Collective intelligence:** This future sees a world where the sum of knowledge and experience of a community leads to better decision-making and problem-solving. Crowdsourcing solutions, co-creation, and collective learning all play a role in how we tackle challenges together.

6. Redefining Leadership and Governance

- **Inclusive leadership:** In a connected future, leadership is more collaborative, transparent, and inclusive. Leaders emerge from communities, not just from top-down systems. The ability to lead with empathy, listening, and accountability becomes critical as communities increasingly rely on shared decision-making processes.

- **Decentralized governance:** Technology enables decentralized systems where decision-making power is distributed among many rather than held by a few. Blockchain, for example, is one technology that offers a vision of governance where decisions are made transparently, and people have a direct say in how things are managed.

7. Education and Lifelong Learning

- **Global learning ecosystems:** In a connected future, access to education isn't confined to traditional classrooms. With digital learning platforms, online courses, and virtual schools, anyone, anywhere, can learn and grow. This means creating learning ecosystems that are adaptive, accessible, and inclusive, allowing people to continuously upskill and reskill in response to changing needs.
- **Collaborative learning:** Education in this future will be more about collaboration than competition. Communities of learners will work together to share knowledge, tackle problems, and innovate in ways that drive collective growth. The value of peer learning and mentorship will be amplified, with individuals supporting each other in their educational journeys.

8. Empowering Individuals to Drive Change

- **Personal empowerment:** A connected future places value on empowering individuals to take action. Whether it's through entrepreneurship, activism, or community-building, everyone should have the tools and support to make a difference in the world. Access to resources, knowledge, and networks should be democratized, allowing people to initiate and drive change on their own terms.

- **Decentralized impact:** Instead of waiting for large organizations or governments to solve problems, individuals and small groups will play a key role in driving social and environmental impact. By harnessing the power of networks and technology, anyone can create ripple effects that lead to large-scale change.

9. Fostering Well-Being and Mental Health

- **Mental health integration:** As communities become more connected, mental health should be prioritized. Creating spaces where people can talk about their mental health, share resources, and support each other is vital. Technology can also help in mental health care by providing access to therapy, self-care resources, and emotional support networks.
- **Work-life harmony:** A connected future means embracing a new approach to work-life balance. Remote work, flexible schedules, and a focus on well-being will be central to a connected society where personal and professional lives can coexist more harmoniously.

10. Sustainability and Intergenerational Responsibility

- **Environmental stewardship:** A connected future also places a high priority on sustainability, ensuring that we leave a world better than we found it. This vision involves using resources

responsibly, protecting ecosystems, and taking collective action to combat climate change.
- **Intergenerational bonds:** Communities of the future will prioritize creating legacies that are passed down through generations. This involves not just preserving the environment, but fostering shared values, culture, and history that can be celebrated and built upon.

In conclusion, visioning a connected future is about imagining a world where individuals, organizations, and societies are united through shared values, technology, empathy, and collaboration. It's about creating a world where barriers—whether physical, emotional, or cultural—are broken down, and the collective potential of humanity is unleashed for a better, more sustainable, and equitable future. This vision is built on the belief that together, we can shape a future that is stronger, more compassionate, and more connected than ever before.

Manifesto for Builders of Belonging in Communities

A Manifesto for Builders of Belonging in Community

We, the builders of belonging, stand united in our commitment to creating communities where every individual is seen, valued, and empowered. We believe that true belonging is not just a feeling, but a collective action—an ongoing, intentional process of nurturing connections, fostering empathy, and celebrating diversity. This manifesto is a declaration of our shared values, principles, and the path we pledge to walk together to build spaces where people can thrive and grow.

1. We Believe in the Power of Inclusion

- **Every voice matters.** We understand that belonging is rooted in the inclusion of all people, regardless of their background, identity, or beliefs. We celebrate the unique contributions that each individual brings to the table and strive to create spaces where everyone feels safe, respected, and heard.
- **Access to participation is a right.** We will break down barriers to entry, ensuring that no one is excluded from our community based on their race, gender, socioeconomic status, or other factors that limit access. We commit to removing obstacles and creating pathways for everyone to participate.

2. We Foster Connection Through Empathy

- **We listen to understand.** True connection begins with deep empathy. We will take the time to listen—without judgment, without agenda—so that we can truly understand each other's experiences, needs, and dreams. We will create spaces where vulnerability is met with support and where differences are celebrated as opportunities for learning.
- **We share our humanity.** We believe that to build belonging, we must be authentic. We will lead with our own stories, allowing others to feel safe in sharing theirs. Our communities are stronger when we embrace our shared humanity and approach each other with kindness and understanding.

3. We Prioritize Mutual Respect and Trust

- **We build relationships on trust.** We understand
  that trust is the foundation of any meaningful
  community. We commit to being transparent,
  honest, and consistent in our actions. Trust is
  earned, and we will work every day to maintain it
  through integrity, respect, and accountability.
- **We treat each other with respect.** Our
  differences are not obstacles; they are
  opportunities for growth. We will honor each
  person's dignity, voice, and perspective. Our
  community will be one where disagreement is
  handled with respect, and diversity of thought is
  embraced as a source of strength.

4. We Cultivate Empowerment and Agency

- **We lift each other up.** We believe that true
  belonging empowers people to be their best selves.
  We will create environments where individuals
  feel inspired and capable of contributing to the
  community. We will provide the tools, resources,
  and support that allow everyone to thrive, no
  matter their background or experience.
- **We amplify the voices of the unheard.** We will
  actively seek out and amplify voices that have
  historically been marginalized. We believe that
  leadership should come from all corners of the
  community, and we will create opportunities for
  everyone to lead, regardless of their status or
  position.

5. We Embrace Change and Growth

- **We are committed to continuous learning.** We
  understand that building a community of

belonging requires constant evolution. We will
never stop learning from each other, adapting to
new challenges, and growing as individuals and as
a collective. We will cultivate a growth mindset,
where mistakes are seen as opportunities to learn
and improve.

- **We honor progress, not perfection.** We believe
that the process of building belonging is ongoing
and imperfect. We will celebrate progress, even in
small steps, and understand that every effort
contributes to the greater vision. We will remain
humble and open to feedback, knowing that there
is always more to learn and do.

6. We Build with Intentionality and Purpose

- **We create with intention.** Our communities are
not built by chance. We will approach every
aspect of community-building with intention, from
the spaces we create to the values we uphold. We
will be clear about our mission, goals, and actions,
ensuring that everything we do supports the goal
of fostering belonging.
- **We act with purpose.** Each decision we make
will be guided by a commitment to building a
community where belonging is a foundational
principle. We will never compromise on this
purpose, even when faced with challenges or
resistance.

7. We Nurture Collaborative Spirit

- **We create together.** We understand that
belonging is a collective effort. We will build
communities where collaboration is the norm, not
the exception. Every member will be encouraged
to contribute their unique talents, perspectives, and

energies to create something greater than any one individual could achieve alone.

- **We celebrate shared success.** We recognize that the success of one is the success of all. We will celebrate collective achievements, big and small, and ensure that everyone shares in the joy of what we create together. We will lift each other up in times of success and offer support in times of challenge.

8. We Commit to Justice and Equity

- **We act with fairness.** We are committed to creating communities where justice and equity are fundamental. We will address systemic inequalities and biases, actively working to dismantle structures that perpetuate discrimination and exclusion. Our community will be one where fairness and equal opportunity are foundational principles.
- **We embrace accountability.** We hold ourselves accountable to our mission of creating a truly inclusive, equitable community. We will challenge ourselves and others to stay true to these principles, ensuring that our actions align with our values.

9. We Celebrate Belonging as a Universal Need

- **We believe in the universal desire for belonging.** Every individual, regardless of background or experience, has an innate need to belong. We will create spaces where people are welcomed and embraced for who they are, not for what they can do or give. We believe that everyone deserves to experience the warmth, connection, and acceptance that belonging offers.

- **We recognize the transformative power of belonging.** We know that when people feel they truly belong, they can unleash their full potential. We commit to nurturing this transformative power, helping individuals grow, connect, and contribute to the well-being of the larger community.

10. We Lead with Love and Compassion

- **We act from a place of love.** Building belonging is an act of love. We will approach every interaction with compassion, care, and generosity. We understand that love creates the foundation for deep, lasting connections and that it is the greatest force in building meaningful, thriving communities.
- **We nurture each other.** We will hold space for each other's growth and well-being, understanding that true belonging is about more than just fitting in—it's about helping one another flourish. We will foster communities where empathy, kindness, and compassion are the pillars that hold us up.

Together, we stand as builders of belonging, committed to creating spaces where every individual has the opportunity to thrive. We pledge to nurture, protect, and expand the circle of belonging, ensuring that it remains a source of strength, unity, and growth for all. Through our actions, we will transform our communities into places where connection, understanding, and mutual care flourish, paving the way for a brighter, more inclusive future.

SECTION 5

The UnityCircle Strategy Framework

How UnityCircle is building an ecosystem with ERG (Community) Strategy

A strong **community strategy** for UnityCircle should reflect its dual role as a **platform for ERGs** and as a **community operating system**. Your strategy should align with three core pillars:

UnityCircle Community Strategy Framework

1. Structure: Build a Scalable ERG Ecosystem

Establish strong foundations that allow ERGs to thrive independently while contributing to the broader community.

Key Actions:

- Define ERG lifecycle stages: *create → grow → sustain → measure*
- Offer templated structures for onboarding, leadership, goals, and budgets
- Support cross-functional and cross-company ERG collaboration
- Enable role-based access: Admins, Leaders, Members, Sponsors

---

2. Engagement: Foster a Vibrant, Inclusive Culture

Create spaces where users feel seen, valued, and motivated to participate regularly.

Key Actions:

- Build engagement loops: content → feedback → recognition
- Personalize user feeds based on interests and identities
- Enable rituals: welcome posts, ERG anniversary badges, shoutouts
- Integrate gamification (leaderboards, points, spotlighting contributions)

---

3. Impact: Align Community Activity with Business Value

Ensure ERGs contribute to measurable DEI, engagement, and business goals.

Key Actions:

- Offer dashboards: ERG activity, member growth, DEI impact
- Support reporting tools for HR, DEI, and leadership
- Promote ERG-led initiatives that align with company OKRs
- Map engagement to business metrics (retention, satisfaction, innovation)

Strategic Objectives

Goal	How UnityCircle Delivers
Build Belonging	Community-driven spaces, intersectional ERG networks
Scale ERG Leadership	ERG leader training, templates, AI nudges
Enable Allyship	Educational content, opt-in to ally roles across ERGs
Strengthen Visibility	Event promotion tools, featured stories, user spotlights
Track & Improve DEI Outcomes	Analytics, engagement heatmaps, integration with HR systems

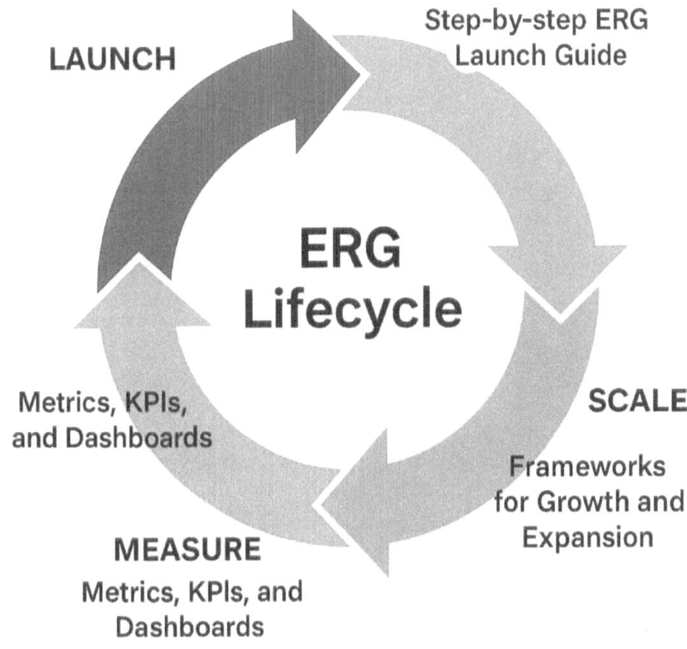

How do we engage People into the Communities (ERGs)?

Creating an ERG is just the beginning—**sustained engagement** is what truly brings it to life. Employees won't automatically participate unless they feel **invited, inspired, and empowered** to do so.

 The key question isn't just *"How do we form a community?"*

It's: **"How do we make people *want* to be part of it?"**

Here are proven strategies to engage employees meaningfully:

---

1. Start with *Why*

Help employees understand the purpose of the ERG—not just what it does, but **why it matters** to them personally.

People join when they see that the community reflects their identity, values, or goals.

- Share the ERG's mission in relatable, human terms
- Communicate how it impacts personal wellbeing and career growth

---

2. Create Psychological Safety First

Before people show up, they must feel it's **safe to show up**.
That means fostering a space where they won't be judged, excluded, or tokenized.

- Invite participation without pressure
- Encourage vulnerability through storytelling and shared experiences
- Promote allyship as a core value

---

3. Design for Inclusion, Not Just Diversity

A group isn't inclusive just because it's open—it's inclusive when **everyone feels they belong**.

- Use inclusive language in all communication
- Provide multiple ways to engage (events, Slack groups, storytelling walls, anonymous surveys)
- Rotate facilitators or leaders to share space and voice

4. Make It Social, Not Just Functional

People crave **connection**, not another task on their calendar.

- Host informal gatherings, fun events, and themed months
- Use micro-moments (coffee chats, walk-and-talks, peer shout-outs)
- Celebrate small wins and people stories regularly

5. Give Ownership and Visibility

Let employees **co-create** the community with you.
People engage more when they feel **it's theirs**, not just HR's or leadership's.

- Invite volunteers to lead initiatives
- Highlight ERG contributions during all-hands or town halls
- Showcase ERG members in internal newsletters or LinkedIn

6. Keep the Engagement Loop Alive

Consistent communication and feedback are crucial.

- Share progress and impact stories regularly
- Ask for feedback—and act on it
- Let members help shape the roadmap

Final Thought

People don't join communities—they join causes, stories, and relationships.

The more human, authentic, and participatory your ERG is, the more people will feel drawn to it.
Engagement is not about invitation. It's about inspiration.

How Communities Shaped Civilizations

Communities have **shaped civilizations** by being the fundamental building blocks through which humans organized themselves, shared knowledge, created culture, and solved problems collectively. Without communities, civilization as we know it could not have emerged.

How Communities Shaped Civilizations

1. Survival and Social Evolution

- Early human groups formed **tribal communities** for safety, hunting, and sharing resources.
- Cooperation and shared norms laid the foundation for **language, rituals, and social contracts**.

2. Formation of Settlements

- Communities evolved from nomadic bands into **agricultural villages**.
- Shared labor and resource pooling enabled **permanent homes, irrigation, and food storage**.
- Settlements grew into **cities and city-states**—the roots of civilizations.

3. Knowledge and Culture Transmission

- Communities passed down **oral traditions, stories, and values**.
- They created **education systems**, guilds, and places of worship.
- Collective memory allowed the **preservation of language, laws, and identity**.

4. Governance and Justice

- Communities organized around **rules, leaders, and social norms**.
- Justice systems, councils, and democratic models **emerged from local decision-making**.

5. Innovation and Infrastructure

- Public works (roads, aqueducts, granaries) were built through **collective effort**.

- Communities drove **technological innovation** in farming, metallurgy, medicine, and more.

6. Trade and Global Networks

- Inter-community interaction led to **exchange of goods, ideas, and culture**.
- Civilizations grew by connecting through **trade routes**, religious pilgrimages, and exploration.

7. Spiritual and Ethical Systems

- Shared beliefs within communities formed **religions and moral codes**.
- These created **identity and cohesion** across large populations and empires.

Big Idea:

Communities weren't just part of civilization — they *were* civilization. From kinship clans to modern cities, from religious orders to online networks, the community has always been humanity's greatest technology.

Tribes to Town – in terms of Community Evolution

The evolution of communities from **tribes to towns** is a story of human adaptation, cooperation, and innovation. It reflects how people moved from **survival-driven groups** to **complex societies** capable of building infrastructure, culture, and governance.

How Communities Evolved: From Tribes to Towns

1. Tribal Communities (Prehistoric Era)

Small, nomadic, kin-based groups

- **Size**: 20–150 people
- **Economy**: Hunting, gathering
- **Structure**: Egalitarian or elder-led; oral tradition
- **Purpose**: Survival, kinship, safety

Key Community Traits:

- Shared language, rituals, and territory
- Cooperation for food and protection
- Deep emotional and spiritual bonds

---

2. Agricultural Settlements (Neolithic Revolution)

The shift to farming changed everything (~10,000 years ago)

- **Innovation**: Domestication of plants and animals
- **Lifestyle**: Sedentary life replaces nomadic
- **Population growth**: Enabled by food surplus
- **Property**: Emergence of ownership, land claims

Result:

- Villages form near rivers and fertile plains
- Division of labor begins (farmers, toolmakers, healers)

3. Permanent Villages and Proto-Towns

Social complexity grows

- Construction of **permanent homes** (mud, stone, wood)
- Development of **local economies**, markets
- Birth of **clans, castes, and roles** (e.g., leaders, artisans)
- Use of **pottery, weaving, metal tools**

Key community leap:

- Shared infrastructure: granaries, wells, walls
- Early community decision-making, councils

4. Towns and City-States (Bronze Age onward)

Urbanization begins (~3000 BCE)

- Larger populations, centralized leadership
- Development of **writing, record-keeping, trade systems**
- Organized religion and **civic spaces** (temples, forums)
- Construction of walls, roads, aqueducts

Community becomes Civilization:

- People no longer know everyone personally — **shared identity now through symbols, stories, and laws**
- Rise of **governance, taxes, law codes, education**

Summary:

- **Tribes**: Small, mobile, survival-driven
- **Villages**: Settled, agrarian, kin-based
- **Towns**: Structured, diverse, innovation-driven

Each stage added **new layers of social organization**, enabling cooperation across greater numbers of people.

What are the ways to make employees happy?

Creating a happy workforce isn't just about perks—it's about building a **genuinely fulfilling, respectful, and engaging environment**. Here are **proven ways** to make employees happy at work, categorized into key pillars:

---

1. Psychological Safety & Belonging

- Promote **open communication** without fear of judgment.
- Encourage **inclusivity and diversity** in team discussions.
- Actively support **Employee Resource Groups (ERGs)** for community and connection.

---

2. Growth & Recognition

- Provide **clear career paths**, mentorship, and upskilling opportunities.

- Offer regular **feedback and recognition** (peer and manager-based).
- Celebrate small and big wins (birthdays, work anniversaries, project milestones).

---

3. Purpose & Autonomy

- Help employees understand how their work ties into the **company's mission**.
- Give them **ownership of projects**, with trust and space to experiment.
- Involve them in **decision-making** when appropriate.

---

4. Work-Life Balance & Flexibility

- Offer **flexible working hours** and **remote work options**.
- Enforce **healthy boundaries** (no weekend emails, promote time off).
- Support with **mental health resources**, counseling, or wellbeing days.

---

5. Fair Compensation & Benefits

- Ensure salaries are **competitive and transparent**.
- Provide **health insurance**, parental leave, and retirement plans.
- Include **non-monetary benefits** like wellness programs, gym subsidies, etc.

---

6. Great Tools & Work Environment

- Provide tools that reduce friction (e.g., modern HR platforms, collaboration software).
- Invest in **ergonomic and aesthetic office spaces**.
- Ensure team rituals—daily standups, all-hands, feedback sessions—are meaningful.

7. Culture of Empathy & Leadership

- Train managers on **emotional intelligence** and people-first leadership.
- Create an **empathy-first culture**—check-ins, active listening, and understanding personal contexts.
- Prioritize **transparency from leadership**—about business, challenges, and wins.

What are the Contributing Factors to Workplace Happiness among Employees by Age

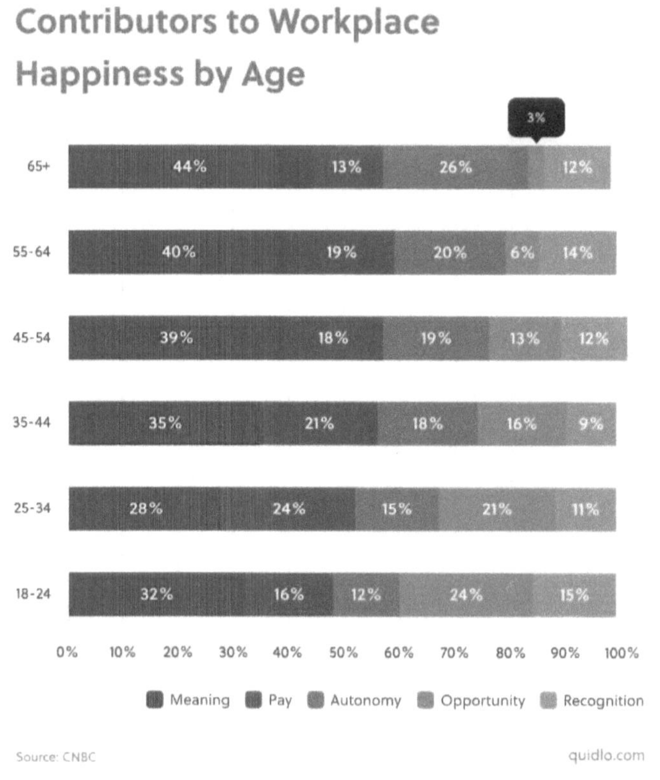

I have been staring at this stats for sometime and I thought there is great learning from this -

Every company needs to be purposeful and providing meaningful role and work for employees. The narratives have to be tweaked to be more purposeful - good for marketing and also for retention of the employees. The weight of this factor seems to be increasing, as the age increases.

Pay matters only during middle age, clearly and not a significant factor overall, compared to others. Pay and Meaning fights (push and pull) in the middle age, clearly! :-)

Autonomy and Freedom is what every human being expects and would like to be lavishly provided to make them feel responsible, proactive, accountable. This can be achieved only by providing them the ownership in what the employees do. This is always constant.

Opportunity factor diminishes after 50, but until then it is a matter of concern for sure, for growth!

Recognition is something every human being needs it. This gets enabled via #EmployeeResourceGroups #ERGs by constant recognitions, triggering #Dopamine and every employee can be kept always #Happy and #Productive.

#Happiness of #Employees is fundamental for the success of the workplace and it is possible by building right #HappyWorkplace #Culture by building #Communities underneath the formal organizations!

Thanks Quidlo for the infographic!

Empowering ERG Leaders with Tools

How to Equip ERG Chairs for Long-Term Success and Impact

Behind every thriving Employee Resource Group (ERG) is a passionate, resilient leader. These individuals are the driving force behind inclusive programming, culture change, and community-building in the workplace. But passion alone isn't sustainable. To build effective, lasting groups, we must empower **ERG leadership** with the right tools, support, and structure.

In this article, we explore how companies can support their **ERG chairs** and leaders with the systems and resources they need to succeed—and avoid burnout along the way.

The Role of ERG Leaders: More Than Volunteers

ERG leaders take on a high-impact role, often on top of their day jobs. Their responsibilities may include:

- Organizing events and campaigns
- Leading team meetings
- Managing budgets
- Reporting on impact and KPIs
- Navigating complex DEI and business landscapes

Without clear support, these tasks can quickly lead to fatigue and frustration. That's why smart organizations invest in **tools for ERG chairs** to make the job easier, more strategic, and more rewarding.

Why ERG Leadership Support Is Non-Negotiable

Strong ERG leadership delivers:

- Better programming and engagement
- Stronger alignment with business goals
- Higher retention and satisfaction for underrepresented employees
- Leadership development for future company influencers

Yet many ERG chairs feel overworked and under-resourced. The solution? Equip them like you would any other leadership role—with training, systems, and support.

7 Essential Tools for ERG Chairs

1. ERG Leadership Playbook

A centralized guide that outlines:

- Roles and responsibilities
- Annual planning templates
- Event planning timelines
- Communication best practices
- Conflict resolution guidance

This removes ambiguity and speeds up onboarding for new leaders.

2. Event & Budget Management Platform

Planning and tracking events is time-consuming. A dedicated platform should allow ERG chairs to:

- Submit event requests
- Track attendance and feedback
- Manage annual budgets and expenses
- Report outcomes to stakeholders

Pro tip: Tools like UnityCircle simplify all of this in one dashboard.

---

3. Membership Engagement Tools

Engagement is the heartbeat of any ERG. Equip chairs with:

- Email and communication tools
- Slack or Teams integration
- Polls and surveys for feedback
- Calendars and RSVP systems

This helps leaders stay connected with their members, especially across remote or global teams.

---

4. Leadership Development Resources

ERG chairs are potential future leaders. Offer them:

- Executive coaching or mentorship
- Access to leadership workshops
- Recognition in performance reviews
- DEI and inclusive leadership training

Companies like Accenture and Salesforce formalize these programs to ensure ERG roles are stepping stones—not dead ends.

5. KPI Dashboards and Reporting Tools

Showcasing impact builds credibility. ERG chairs need simple ways to:

- Track event reach
- Measure member participation
- Capture feedback
- Tie outcomes to DEI or business KPIs

Tip: ERG dashboards should be easy to update and share with leadership.

6. Cross-ERG Collaboration Hub

Many ERGs overlap in goals or audience. Provide a space for leaders to:

- Share best practices
- Co-host events
- Solve common challenges together
- Avoid duplication of efforts

A shared workspace fosters innovation and consistency across your entire ERG ecosystem.

7. Executive Access and Sponsorship Tools

Ensure ERG chairs have visibility with decision-makers:

- Set up regular sponsor meetings
- Provide agenda templates
- Track executive involvement
- Enable upward reporting to DEI councils or HR

Leaders who feel heard and supported are more likely to sustain their energy and impact.

The Future of ERG Leadership Starts with Support

If ERGs are the future of workplace inclusion, **ERG chairs** are the architects of that future. Investing in their success isn't just a "nice to have"—it's a business imperative.

Empowered ERG leaders:

- Drive real cultural transformation
- Build inclusive talent pipelines
- Create safer, more connected workplaces

UnityCircle: The Platform Built for ERG Leaders

At **UnityCircle**, we know that ERG leadership requires heart *and* structure. That's why our platform is designed to give ERG chairs everything they need:

- Customizable ERG playbooks
- Budget and event tools
- Member engagement insights
- KPI tracking dashboards
- Leadership training resources

Want to support your ERG leaders the right way?
Book a demo with UnityCircle and start building a stronger, more scalable ERG program.

The Role of ERGs in Employee Retention

How Employee Resource Groups Strengthen Engagement and Reduce Turnover

Employee turnover is one of the most costly challenges organizations face. In a competitive job market, retaining top talent is more than a matter of salary—it's about creating a culture where employees feel seen, valued, and connected. That's where **Employee Resource Groups (ERGs)** come in.

In this article, we explore the powerful link between **ERGs and retention**, and how these employee-led groups have become essential **employee engagement tools** for forward-thinking companies.

Why Retention Matters More Than Ever

Hiring new talent can cost up to 200% of an employee's salary, depending on the role. But beyond financial cost, high turnover disrupts teams, stalls innovation, and damages culture.

Today's employees—especially Gen Z and Millennials—seek workplaces where they can bring their full selves to work. Belonging, community, and purpose are top priorities. ERGs deliver all three.

How ERGs Help Retain Talent

1. Fostering a Sense of Belonging

ERGs provide safe spaces for employees with shared backgrounds, interests, or identities. They help people feel:

- Seen and supported
- Connected to colleagues with similar experiences
- Validated in their unique perspectives

This sense of belonging is directly tied to retention—employees who feel included are more likely to stay.

A 2023 Culture Amp study showed that employees involved in ERGs had 12% higher intent to stay compared to non-members.

---

2. Creating Community and Peer Networks

Work is more than tasks—it's relationships. ERGs help employees build networks that go beyond their immediate team, creating:

- Cross-functional relationships
- Informal mentorship opportunities
- Greater visibility within the organization

When employees have a support system at work, they're less likely to leave in search of a better culture elsewhere.

---

3. Promoting Leadership and Growth

Many ERGs offer leadership roles, speaker opportunities, and access to executive sponsors. These experiences are not only empowering—they also enhance:

- Professional development
- Career visibility
- Confidence and influence

This makes ERGs a practical **employee engagement tool** for developing future leaders, especially those from underrepresented backgrounds.

---

4. Improving Organizational Trust

ERGs act as two-way communication channels between employees and leadership. By voicing concerns, proposing initiatives, and helping shape inclusive policies, they build trust and transparency.

Employees who trust their employer are significantly more likely to remain long-term.

SECTION 6

How to Launch, Scale and Sustain ERGs

How to Start an ERG in Your Company

Step-by-Step Guide to Launching Employee-Led Groups That Drive Culture and Belonging

In today's dynamic workplaces, **Employee Resource Groups (ERGs)** are no longer optional — they're essential. Whether you're a DEI leader, HR partner, or a passionate employee who wants to build community, you may be wondering: **how do you start an ERG**?

This guide will walk you through the step-by-step process of **how to start an ERG**, turning an idea into an impactful, employee-led group that creates lasting value.

What Is an ERG?

Before we dive in, let's clarify: An **Employee Resource Group (ERG)** is a **voluntary, employee-led group** formed around shared identities, interests, or experiences—such as race, gender, LGBTQ+ identity, parenting, or disability status.

ERGs create safe spaces, build community, and provide a voice for underrepresented or shared-interest employee groups. They're also key to fostering belonging and driving diversity, equity, and inclusion from within.

Why Start an ERG?

Starting an ERG can:

- Promote belonging and psychological safety
- Support career development and mentorship
- Influence inclusive policies and practices
- Create visibility for historically marginalized groups
- Align employees around purpose, identity, and advocacy

In short, ERGs make companies stronger — culturally and competitively.

How to Start an ERG: A Step-by-Step Guide

1. Identify the Need or Shared Identity

Start by listening. Are there employees who feel underrepresented, disconnected, or eager to gather around a shared experience? Whether it's a women's network, a veterans' group, or a sustainability-focused team, the best ERGs are **rooted in real community needs**.

 Tip: Conduct a quick interest survey or host a town hall to test the waters.

---

2. Build a Core Team of Founders

No ERG should be a solo effort. Form a small, committed founding team — ideally with diverse perspectives and energy. This team will shape the group's vision and lead initial operations.

☐ **Look for:**

- A passionate group lead or co-leads
- Members representing the identity or interest
- An executive sponsor (see next step)

---

3. Secure Executive Sponsorship

Having a leader at the table provides your ERG with:

- Visibility and credibility
- Budget support
- A voice in strategic decisions

Choose a sponsor who is committed, available, and willing to advocate for the group at leadership levels.

---

4. Define the ERG's Mission and Goals

Clarity of purpose is key. Define:

- **Who** the ERG serves
- **What** its mission is
- **How** it aligns with company values
- **What success looks like** (events, initiatives, member engagement, etc.)

Example: "To support LGBTQ+ employees by creating safe spaces, educating allies, and influencing inclusive workplace policies."

---

5. Set a Governance Structure

Even employee-led groups need structure to succeed.
Decide:

- Leadership roles (lead, co-leads, committees)
- Meeting cadence
- Decision-making process
- Budget and resources

A lightweight charter or playbook helps keep things on
track and scalable.

---

6. Launch and Promote the ERG

Plan a formal launch to raise awareness and attract
members. Consider:

- A kickoff event or panel
- Internal newsletter feature
- Intranet or Slack channel creation
- Leadership endorsement

Use inclusive language and emphasize that all employees
(including allies) are welcome to join and support.

7. Start Programming and Engagement

Focus on early wins:

- Safe space discussions
- Speaker events
- Cultural celebrations
- Mentorship pairings

Start small but consistent. ERGs grow with momentum.

8. Measure and Share Impact

Track your ERG's growth, engagement, and outcomes:

- Membership numbers
- Event participation
- Feedback from members
- Policy or culture changes influenced

Sharing wins (and lessons learned) helps your ERG stay visible and valued.

ERGs Are More Than Employee-Led Groups — They're Culture Shapers

Starting an ERG may seem daunting at first, but it's one of the most rewarding ways to build a more connected and inclusive workplace. By following these steps, you can transform shared identity into shared impact — and create a community that empowers, educates, and uplifts.

How UnityCircle Can Help

At **UnityCircle**, we help organizations make it easier to start, grow, and measure employee-led groups. From onboarding ERG leads to providing structure, budgeting tools, and impact dashboards, our platform is built for the future of workplace community.

Want to simplify your ERG program? Book a demo with UnityCircle and get started with confidence.

Building a Scalable ERG Program

*How to Move from Passion Projects to a Powerful,
Repeatable ERG Strategy*

Employee Resource Groups (ERGs) have evolved from
grassroots initiatives into essential engines of inclusion,
innovation, and employee engagement. But as
organizations grow and cultures become more complex,
so does the challenge: **how do you go from a few
passionate ERGs to a truly scalable ERG program**?

In this post, we'll explore the blueprint for **scaling
ERGs**—one that balances structure with autonomy, and
strategy with heart.

Why Scale Your ERG Program?

Many companies start with one or two ERGs—often
launched by energized employees who care deeply about
community. But over time, the need for consistency,
equity, and impact tracking becomes clear. Scaling is not
just about more groups; it's about **systematizing support**
so that every ERG can thrive, no matter the size or
location.

A **scalable ERG strategy** helps you:

- Ensure equity across groups
- Maintain leadership continuity
- Simplify governance and compliance
- Measure and grow impact
- Expand DEI across global offices

1. Standardize the Framework, Not the Experience

Scalability doesn't mean sameness. It means giving every ERG the **tools, support, and flexibility** to succeed. Develop a core ERG framework that includes:

- Mission and charter templates
- Roles and responsibilities
- Funding model
- Onboarding process for ERG leads

Let each group personalize their programming while operating within consistent guardrails.

---

2. Invest in Leadership Development

One of the biggest bottlenecks in **scaling ERGs** is burnout and turnover among ERG leads. ERG leadership should be treated as a recognized stretch assignment—not an invisible extra task.

Support your ERG leaders with:

- Leadership training
- Mentorship from senior execs
- Dedicated time (and performance recognition)
- Access to DEI councils or business units

This not only sustains your program—it builds a pipeline of diverse future leaders.

---

3. Centralize Governance While Encouraging Autonomy

A scalable ERG strategy requires the right balance between **central guidance** and **local creativity**. Consider creating a:

- Central DEI or ERG Program Office
- Governance council with reps from each ERG
- Toolkit of best practices and branding assets
- Quarterly check-ins and community-of-practice calls

This provides accountability while nurturing grassroots energy.

4. Align ERGs with Business Goals

To grow sustainably, ERGs must move from siloed groups to **strategic internal partners**. Encourage ERGs to align with:

- Talent acquisition (e.g., partnering on recruitment events)
- Product inclusion and innovation
- Community impact and CSR efforts
- Leadership development programs

When ERGs contribute to real business value, support scales with them.

5. Measure What Matters

Scaling means showing progress. Define KPIs and metrics that capture both quantitative and qualitative ERG success:

- Membership growth
- Event engagement
- Retention rates among ERG members
- Impact stories and testimonials
- Policy or culture changes driven by ERGs

Build a simple dashboard that leadership and ERG leaders can access to inform planning and showcase ROI.

Scaling ERGs: What Not to Do

Avoid these common pitfalls:

- Over-structuring to the point of bureaucracy
- Ignoring the emotional labor of ERG leaders
- Creating uneven support across ERGs
- Measuring only numbers, not impact
- Letting ERGs operate in isolation from core business strategy

A scalable program is not about control—it's about **capacity building and trust**.

UnityCircle: Scaling ERGs with Confidence

At **UnityCircle**, we understand that a great ERG program doesn't happen by accident—it's built intentionally. Our platform helps you:

- Create standardized playbooks for ERG operations
- Onboard and train ERG leaders at scale
- Track engagement and participation across ERGs
- Ensure transparency, governance, and executive visibility

Whether you have 2 ERGs or 20, UnityCircle helps you scale with strategy.

☐ **Want to scale your ERG program without losing its soul?** Book a demo with UnityCircle and start building community at scale.

Final Thoughts

Scaling ERGs isn't about more—it's about better. With the right structure, leadership support, and alignment to company values, your ERG program can go from good to transformational. A solid **ERG strategy** ensures that every employee, everywhere, feels seen, heard, and empowered to lead.

ERG Best Practices from Top Companies

How Leading Organizations Build Thriving Employee Resource Groups

Employee Resource Groups (ERGs) are powerful drivers of culture, inclusion, and innovation—but running them effectively takes more than passion. It takes structure, strategy, and commitment from both employees and leadership.

So what makes an ERG program not just active, but impactful?

In this article, we'll break down **ERG best practices** learned from some of the world's most forward-thinking companies—and share **ERG examples** that are setting the standard.

Why ERGs Matter More Than Ever

As diversity, equity, and inclusion (DEI) take center stage in business strategy, ERGs are becoming foundational to how companies engage their people. They foster community, support underrepresented groups, and influence everything from product design to talent pipelines.

But the difference between a symbolic ERG and a strategic one? **Best practices rooted in experience**.

7 ERG Best Practices from Top Companies

1. Start with a Clear Mission and Charter

Every successful ERG starts with a shared purpose. Top companies help each ERG define:

- A mission aligned with company values
- Short and long-term goals
- Membership guidelines and roles
- Metrics for success

Example:
At **Google**, ERGs are supported by a common charter

template, which ensures consistency while allowing room for each group's unique identity.

---

2. Secure Executive Sponsorship Early

Strong executive sponsors give ERGs visibility, access, and influence. They also help bridge ERGs to broader business goals.

Best Practice: Assign an exec sponsor to each ERG who:

- Actively participates in events
- Advocates for ERG needs at leadership levels
- Mentors ERG leaders

Example:
Intel's ERGs have executive champions who are responsible for quarterly check-ins and reporting ERG insights directly to the C-suite.

---

3. Provide Budget and Operational Support

ERGs need more than enthusiasm—they need resources. Leading companies offer:

- Annual budgets per ERG
- Event planning support
- Tools for virtual collaboration
- Access to a central ERG operations team

Example:
At **Salesforce**, each ERG receives a dedicated budget and access to the "Ohana Floor," a space reserved for community-driven programming.

4. Offer Leadership Development Opportunities

Serving as an ERG lead is a high-impact leadership opportunity. Top companies treat ERG roles as career-advancing, not side gigs.

Best Practice:

- Offer training, coaching, and networking
- Recognize ERG leadership in performance reviews
- Include ERG leaders in company-wide leadership programs

Example:
Accenture provides ERG leads with mentorship from senior leaders and includes ERG impact in their professional development plans.

---

5. Use Data to Drive Decisions

Great ERG programs are data-informed. That includes tracking:

- Membership growth
- Event engagement
- Internal feedback
- Policy changes influenced by ERGs

Example:
Microsoft uses dashboards to visualize ERG performance and tie it to business KPIs like retention and employee satisfaction.

---

6. Create a Community of Practice

Rather than letting ERGs operate in silos, leading companies encourage collaboration across ERGs and geographies.

Best Practice:

- Host quarterly ERG leader summits
- Create shared calendars for events
- Establish mentorship between new and mature ERGs

Example:
Amazon runs a global ERG leader council where representatives share successes, challenges, and innovations across regions.

---

7. Align ERGs with Business Strategy

The most impactful ERGs don't just serve internal culture—they shape the business. Top companies:

- Involve ERGs in product feedback and design
- Partner ERGs with talent acquisition for outreach
- Engage ERGs in customer and community impact

Example:
Netflix's ERGs work with marketing and product teams to advise on inclusive storytelling and representation in content.

Here are some standout **ERG examples** that reflect these best practices:

- **Black Googler Network (Google)** – Active in advocacy, mentorship, and community investment.
- **PRIDE@SAP (SAP)** – One of the largest LGBTQ+ ERGs globally, with strong executive backing.
- **Women at Microsoft (Microsoft)** – Focused on leadership development and pay equity initiatives.
- **VIVA Latinx (Meta)** – Engages Latinx employees and allies in cultural celebrations and business strategy.
- **Veterans@Amazon (Amazon)** – Supports transition to tech careers and influences military-friendly hiring policies.

Final Thoughts: What Makes an ERG Program Truly Great?

The most successful ERG programs:

- Have strong leadership support
- Offer operational consistency with room for creativity
- Tie community to culture—and culture to business

ERGs are not side projects. They are **strategic assets** that fuel innovation, inclusion, and engagement across the organization.

UnityCircle: Helping You Build Best-in-Class ERGs

At **UnityCircle**, we help companies launch, scale, and manage ERG programs that follow these best practices. From governance frameworks to data dashboards and leadership development, our platform is built to support the future of ERGs.

Ready to build your ERG program the right way? Schedule a demo with UnityCircle and start creating community that matters.

ERG Playbook Download

Your Ultimate Guide to Launching and Scaling Employee Resource Groups

Are you ready to launch or enhance Employee Resource Groups (ERGs) in your organization? Whether you're just starting out or looking to refine your existing groups, a comprehensive playbook can make all the difference. That's why we've created the **UnityCircle ERG Playbook**—a step-by-step **ERG launch guide** to help you build thriving, impactful ERGs that drive business success and employee engagement.

In this article, we walk you through the key steps involved in launching and scaling ERGs, and how the **UnityCircle playbook** can serve as your go-to resource for success.

Why You Need an ERG Playbook

Creating successful ERGs isn't just about gathering employees with shared interests or identities. It's about:

- **Aligning ERG activities with business goals** (such as retention, diversity, and leadership development)
- **Engaging employees in meaningful ways** that foster belonging and inclusion
- **Tracking impact** to prove the value of ERGs to leadership and stakeholders

An ERG playbook serves as your roadmap, helping you avoid common pitfalls and providing clarity on how to build, manage, and scale ERGs effectively.

Key Steps for Launching an ERG: The Ultimate **ERG Launch Guide**

Step 1: Define Your ERG's Purpose and Goals

Start by clearly defining the purpose of your ERG. Will it focus on a specific identity (e.g., women in tech, LGBTQIA+ employees) or a common interest (e.g., sustainability)? Establish measurable goals that tie back to your company's DEI (Diversity, Equity, and Inclusion) and overall business strategy.

*Key Takeaways from the **UnityCircle Playbook***:

- **Establish SMART goals** (Specific, Measurable, Achievable, Relevant, Time-bound) for each ERG.
- Ensure alignment with your company's DEI strategy to enhance credibility and impact.

Step 2: Secure Leadership Buy-In and Executive Sponsorship

To give your ERG the support it needs to thrive, secure executive sponsorship. Having an executive champion who is invested in the success of the ERG will help ensure it gets the resources, visibility, and support it deserves.

Key Takeaways:

- **Executive sponsors** can advocate for ERGs at leadership meetings and provide necessary resources.
- ERGs with executive backing are more likely to achieve long-term sustainability.

Step 3: Build an ERG Leadership Team

An ERG is only as strong as its leadership. Form a diverse leadership team that can help steer the group towards its goals and manage day-to-day activities. Consider a team of 3-5 leaders with different skills and backgrounds, ensuring a balance of representation.

Key Takeaways:

- Ensure **clear roles and responsibilities** within the leadership team.
- Leadership development should be a key focus— ERGs are a great way to nurture future leaders in your company.

Step 4: Promote Your ERG and Attract Members

Once the groundwork is laid, it's time to invite employees to join. Effective promotion is key to ensuring you engage a wide range of employees. Use internal communication channels (email, Slack, intranet) to share the mission of the ERG and its benefits.

Key Takeaways:

- Use **internal champions** to spread the word about the ERG and encourage others to join.
- Host **launch events** and offer informational sessions to engage employees from the start.

Step 5: Plan and Execute ERG Activities

Plan a series of engaging activities, events, and initiatives that align with the group's purpose and your broader organizational goals. Activities should be impactful, inclusive, and diverse to keep members engaged.

*Key Takeaways from the **UnityCircle Playbook**:*

- Use **surveys and feedback** to understand member needs and tailor your activities.
- Focus on **community-building** and learning opportunities to ensure long-term engagement.

Step 6: Measure Success and Demonstrate Impact

Finally, it's essential to track the success of your ERG efforts. Whether it's measuring member participation, the impact of initiatives on employee satisfaction, or contributions to your DEI goals, documenting success helps prove the value of ERGs to leadership.

Key Takeaways:

- Use **data analytics** to track engagement, retention, and other key performance indicators.
- Adjust strategies based on feedback and impact measurement to ensure continuous improvement.

Why Download the **UnityCircle Playbook**?

The **UnityCircle ERG Playbook** is designed to give you everything you need to launch a successful ERG program. Here's why it's an essential resource:

1. **Step-by-Step Guidance**: A clear, actionable roadmap to launch and scale ERGs.

2. **Tools and Templates**: Ready-to-use tools for planning events, tracking metrics, and measuring impact.
3. **Best Practices**: Insights from ERG leaders and DEI experts to help you avoid common mistakes.
4. **Measurable Results**: Focus on outcomes that drive employee engagement, retention, and organizational success.

Ready to Launch Your ERG Program?

To get started, **download the UnityCircle ERG Playbook** today! It's your comprehensive guide to building successful, impactful ERGs that drive inclusivity and business growth.

Download the ERG Playbook Now and unlock the tools you need to create thriving employee communities at your organization.

Final Thoughts

An ERG program has the power to change the culture of your organization. By providing employees with a sense of belonging, purpose, and voice, ERGs are crucial for retention, engagement, and diversity. With the **UnityCircle ERG Playbook,** you have the roadmap and tools to launch and scale successful ERGs that make a difference.

Ready to empower your ERGs? Download the playbook and take your first step toward an inclusive workplace today!

How to bring 100% Happiness and Wellbeing with all Employees at workplace?

Employee happiness at the workplace is influenced by a combination of emotional, environmental, and organizational factors. Here are the **key factors**:

1. Meaningful Work

- Feeling that one's work has purpose or impact.
- Alignment with personal values or societal contribution.

2. Positive Relationships

- Supportive team dynamics.
- Respectful colleagues and empathetic managers.
- Opportunities for social connection (e.g., ERGs, team events).

3. Recognition and Appreciation

- Being valued for contributions.
- Regular feedback and celebration of wins—big or small.

4. Career Growth and Learning

- Access to training, mentorship, and upskilling.
- Clear pathways for advancement.

5. Work-Life Balance

- Reasonable workloads.
- Flexible hours, remote work options, and understanding of personal needs.

6. Psychological Safety

- Freedom to express ideas or concerns without fear.
- Inclusive culture where diverse voices are welcomed.

7. Fair Compensation and Benefits

- Competitive pay, health benefits, and other perks.
- Transparent and equitable reward systems.

8. Autonomy and Trust

- Empowerment to make decisions.
- Minimal micromanagement and trust in ability.

9. Healthy Work Environment

- Ergonomic spaces, good lighting, clean facilities.
- Attention to mental health and wellness resources.

10. Organizational Culture and Values

- Strong, authentic DEI initiatives.
- Leadership that walks the talk.

Tracking **value-generating metrics** in ERG (Employee Resource Group) software is critical to demonstrating the impact of ERGs on employee engagement, DEI (Diversity, Equity & Inclusion) outcomes, and business performance. Here's a comprehensive list of **quantitative and qualitative metrics** you can track and analyze:

Full List of Possible ERGs

1. Identity-Based ERGs

- Women's Network / Women in Leadership
- LGBTQIA+ Network / Pride ERG
- Black or African Heritage Network
- Latinx / Hispanic Heritage Network
- Asian / Pacific Islander Network
- Indigenous / Native American Network
- Middle Eastern and North African (MENA) Network
- Multicultural / Global Ethnicities Network
- People of Color ERG (broad)
- Immigrants and Newcomers Network
- Veterans / Military Service Members Network
- Differently Abled / Disability Inclusion Network
- Neurodiversity Network (e.g., Autism, ADHD support)
- Generational Groups (e.g., Gen Z, Millennials, Gen X, Boomers)
- Parents and Caregivers Network
- Working Moms Network
- Fathers at Work Network
- Single Parents Network

---

2. Belief and Affiliation-Based ERGs

- Faith/Interfaith Networks (e.g., Christian, Muslim, Hindu, Buddhist groups)
- Spirituality and Wellness Groups
- Intercultural Dialogue Networks

3. Life Stage and Well-being ERGs

- Mental Health & Wellness Advocates
- Chronic Illness or Health Conditions Support (e.g., Cancer Survivors Network)
- Bereavement Support Networks
- Addiction Recovery Support Groups
- Retirement Planning or Pre-Retirement Groups

4. Professional Development ERGs

- Early Career / Young Professionals Network
- Emerging Leaders Network
- Mid-Career Professionals Network
- Women in Tech / Minorities in Tech
- Innovation & Entrepreneurship Networks
- First-Generation Professionals Network

5. Cause-Based and Interest-Based ERGs

- Sustainability / Green Teams
- Community Impact / Volunteering Groups
- Social Justice & Advocacy Groups
- Accessibility Advocates
- Animal Welfare Advocates

- Tech Enthusiasts / Coding Clubs
- Remote and Hybrid Workers Network
- Sports and Fitness Clubs
- Book Clubs, Arts and Culture Networks

Special-Purpose and Intersectional ERGs

Some companies create ERGs that **combine identities** or **focus on intersections**, such as:

- Women of Color Network
- LGBTQIA+ People of Color Network
- Veterans with Disabilities Network
- Working Parents of Special Needs Children
- Global Mobility / Expat Employee Networks

⬡ Key Trends (2024–2025)

- **Men as Allies ERGs** (e.g., men supporting gender equity)
- **Socioeconomic Mobility ERGs** (first-gen, low-income backgrounds)
- **Climate Justice ERGs** (linking environmental and DEI activism)
- **Neurodiversity Champions** are rapidly growing
- **Remote-First Worker ERGs** post-pandemic

Important Tip:
Modern companies allow ERGs to be **employee-driven** — meaning if a group of employees sees a shared experience, need, or passion, they can propose a new ERG with leadership support.

1. Women's Network / Women in Leadership ERG

- Focus: Gender equity, leadership development, mentorship.
- Why: Gender diversity is a universal corporate priority and a strong first step in DEI efforts.

2. LGBTQIA+ Network / Pride ERG

- Focus: Creating an inclusive environment for LGBTQIA+ employees and allies.
- Why: Highly visible, fosters psychological safety, and signals clear corporate values.

3. Multicultural / Racial & Ethnic Diversity ERG

- Focus: Support for employees from different racial, ethnic, and cultural backgrounds.
- Why: Helps drive inclusion for a broad population (often broken down into more focused ERGs later).

4. Veterans and Military Families ERG

- Focus: Transition support, mentorship, community building for veterans and their families.
- Why: Shows commitment to honoring service and taps into leadership and resilience skills.

5. Disability Inclusion / Accessibility ERG

- Focus: Supporting employees with disabilities (visible and invisible), accessibility initiatives.

- Why: Promotes workplace accessibility, universal design, and inclusion.

6. Young Professionals / Early Career ERG

- Focus: Professional growth, networking, mentorship for new and early-career employees.
- Why: Builds retention and loyalty among younger talent, who value community and development.

7. Parents and Caregivers ERG

- Focus: Support for working parents, caregivers of elders or special needs individuals.
- Why: Addresses a very real challenge in work-life balance and boosts retention across genders.

Optional Add-Ons (depending on company size and culture)

- Mental Health and Wellness ERG
- Sustainability / Green Team
- Faith or Interfaith Network
- Remote and Hybrid Workers ERG (especially important post-COVID)

Pro Tip for Launch

Instead of launching everything at once, many companies:

- **Start with 3–4 ERGs** based on employee interest.
- Provide each group with **basic structure + small budget**.

- Encourage **intersectional partnerships** (e.g., Women's Network and LGBTQ+ Network co-hosting events).
- Gradually expand based on engagement and company priorities.

⬚ Sample ERG Rollout Plan (6–9 Months)

Executive Sponsorship

- Identify an executive champion for the overall ERG program.
- Encourage individual exec sponsors for each ERG later.

Define ERG Policy and Framework

- Create a basic ERG charter template (purpose, goals, governance).
- Define eligibility for ERG leads (volunteers, term limits if any).
- Decide on initial annual budget per ERG (e.g., $5K–$15K per group).

Communications Plan

- Prepare messaging: why ERGs, leadership support, and how employees can get involved.
- Set launch timeline expectations publicly.

Employee Interest Survey

- Short survey to assess employee interest in ERGs and preferred themes.
- Include option for employees to suggest new ERGs.

Recruit ERG Founders and Leaders

- Open calls for ERG leaders/founders.
- Select passionate individuals willing to help build ERGs.

Initial ERG Registration

- Formalize the first 3–5 ERGs based on survey data + strategic priorities.
- Help each ERG draft a simple charter (mission, objectives, leadership team).

ERG Leader Training

- Quick leadership onboarding (90-minute session on how to run events, manage budget, report metrics).

Kick-off Events

- Each ERG hosts a virtual or in-person launch event.

- Showcase leadership support: CEO/execs attend and give short speeches.
- Invite membership sign-ups during events.

Budget Activation

- Disburse small starter budgets.
- Encourage quick wins: lunches, small networking events, webinars, panels.

Internal Marketing

- Regular newsletters, Slack channels, intranet pages to promote ERG activities.

Set KPIs

- Track participation numbers, event attendance, volunteer engagement, and feedback.

Phase 4: Full Activation and Growth (Month 6–9)

Signature Events

- Encourage each ERG to host 1–2 major events tied to calendar moments (e.g., Pride Month, Women's History Month).

Cross-ERG Collaboration

- Foster partnerships between ERGs for intersectional events (e.g., "Women of Color in Leadership" panel).

Feedback Loop

- Mid-year pulse surveys to measure engagement and improvement ideas.
- Create quarterly reporting templates for ERG leaders (successes, challenges, requests).

Recognition

- Publicly recognize ERG leads and active members.
- Offer small awards or acknowledgments to sustain momentum.

Visual Timeline (Quick View)

Month	Activities
1–2	Executive sponsorship, policies, communication plan
2–4	Interest surveys, recruit leaders, form ERGs, leader training
4–6	Soft launch events, activate budgets, internal marketing
6–9	Signature events, cross-ERG collaborations, feedback, recognition

---

Result by Month 9:
You'll have a visible, structured, and employee-driven ERG program with measurable early impact and strong leadership support.

Sample ERG Charter Template

1. ERG Name

- What is the official name of your ERG?
- (Tip: Keep it inclusive and clear — e.g., "Pride Network," "Women in Leadership," "Veterans Connect.")

2. Mission Statement

- 2–3 sentences explaining **why the ERG exists**.
- Example:

> "The Pride Network exists to foster an inclusive environment where LGBTQIA+ employees and allies feel supported, celebrated, and empowered to thrive personally and professionally."

3. Objectives and Goals

List 3–5 **key goals** the ERG will focus on for the year. Examples:

- Build a supportive community for members.
- Host professional development and networking events.
- Advocate for inclusive company policies and practices.
- Partner with recruiting to support diversity hiring.
- Support company culture initiatives (e.g., DEI training, volunteering).

4. Membership

- **Eligibility:** Open to all employees? (Strongly recommended.)
- **Expectations:** Clarify that participation is voluntary and open to allies.

5. Leadership Structure

- List initial ERG leaders (names and roles):
    - Chair/Co-Chairs
    - Communications Lead
    - Events Lead
    - Membership Engagement Lead
    - Executive Sponsor (assigned by leadership)

(Note: Small ERGs can start with just a Chair and an Executive Sponsor!)

6. Executive Sponsor

- Name of the assigned executive sponsor.
- Sponsor Role:
    - Advocate for the ERG at leadership level.
    - Attend key events.
    - Help unlock resources and visibility.

7. Planned Activities

- Examples:
    - Monthly networking meetups.
    - Speaker series or panels.
    - Community service projects.
    - Company-wide awareness campaigns (Pride Month, Black History Month, etc.).
    - Mentorship programs.

8. Budget

- Proposed annual budget (if applicable) and a rough plan for usage.
- Examples: Event hosting, marketing materials, guest speakers, volunteering logistics.

9. Measurement of Success

- How will you track your impact? Examples:
    - Number of members and event attendees.
    - Member satisfaction surveys.
    - Contributions to company DEI goals (e.g., recruiting, retention, policy changes).
    - Testimonials or stories shared by members.

10. Review and Renewal

- Charter reviewed annually with DEI/HR team.
- Update goals and leadership annually or bi-annually.

Pro Tip for You:
Keep the charter **short — 2–3 pages max**. The goal is to empower employees, **not to overcomplicate** the process with bureaucracy.

One-Page Quick ERG Charter Template

ERG Name:

(Enter the name of your group)

Mission Statement:

(One or two sentences describing the purpose of the ERG)

Key Goals (Top 3 for this Year):

1.
2.
3.

Leadership Team:

- Chair/Co-Chair: ______________________________
- Communications Lead (optional): ______________________________
- Executive Sponsor: ______________________________

Membership:

- Open to: *(e.g., all employees, specific affinity group + allies)*

Planned Signature Activities:

(List 2–3 major events, programs, or initiatives you plan to host)

Success Metrics:

(How you will measure success — e.g., membership growth, event attendance, feedback surveys)

Budget Estimate (if needed):

(Rough number or range if requesting a budget — e.g., $3,000 for events)

Important Tip:
"Start simple, grow later." — The charter can always be expanded once the ERG is active and learns what members want most.

Sample One-Page ERG Charter

ERG Name:
Women in Leadership Network (WILN)

Mission Statement:
To empower, connect, and advance women at all career
stages by creating opportunities for mentorship,
leadership development, and advocacy within the
organization.

Key Goals (Top 3 for this Year):

1. Host quarterly leadership development workshops
   for women employees.
2. Launch a mentorship program connecting
   emerging women leaders with senior executives.
3. Celebrate International Women's Day with a
   company-wide event and speaker panel.

Leadership Team:

- Chair: Priya Sharma
- Communications Lead: Anita Joseph
- Executive Sponsor: Rajiv Menon, Chief
  Marketing Officer

Membership:
Open to all employees who identify as women, nonbinary
individuals, and allies.

Planned Signature Activities:

- "Women Who Lead" quarterly speaker series.
- Launch a 6-month mentorship program (pilot with 20 mentor/mentee pairs).
- International Women's Day keynote and networking event.

Success Metrics:

- 150 members by year-end.
- 75% satisfaction rating in post-event surveys.
- 20 mentorship pairs successfully matched and completing the program.

Budget Estimate (if needed): $7,500 for speaker fees, event logistics, marketing materials, and mentorship kickoff event.

How it Helps:
This example shows that filling out the quick charter is easy, clear, and action-focused — without overwhelming new ERG leaders.

Professional Looking ERG Charter

[Your Company Logo]

ERG Charter Template

ERG Name:

Mission Statement:

(Briefly describe the purpose and vision of the ERG.)

Key Goals for the Year:

(List 3 key focus areas.)

1.
2.
3.

Leadership Team:

Role	Name Email
Chair / Co-Chairs	
Communications Lead	
Events Lead	
Executive Sponsor	

Membership:

- Open to: *(e.g., employees who identify with [group] and their allies.)*

Planned Signature Activities:

(Examples: events, mentorship programs, campaigns.)

Success Metrics:

(How you'll measure impact — e.g., number of events, member participation, satisfaction surveys.)

Budget Estimate (if applicable):

(Total budget requested and major spending categories.)

Notes or Special Requests:

(Optional: Anything the ERG needs leadership support with.)

Instructions for ERG Leaders:

- Keep the mission short and inspiring.
- Focus on 2–3 realistic goals for the first year.
- Activities should connect to company values or business goals.
- Update this charter annually.

ERG Launch Checklist

Here is a practical and professional **ERG (Employee Resource Group) Launch Checklist** that you can use when helping companies launch an ERG program or community from scratch:

ERG Launch Checklist

Stage	Action Item	Status
1. Define Purpose & Scope	Identify the business need or employee interest for the ERG	☐
	Define ERG mission, vision, and goals	☐

Stage	Action Item	Status
	Align with company DEI or culture strategy	☐
2. Executive Sponsorship	Secure an executive sponsor or leadership champion	☐
	Define the sponsor's role and involvement expectations	☐
3. Governance Structure	Establish ERG leadership roles (Chair, Co-Chair, etc.)	☐
	Create a charter or guiding document	☐
	Decide on meeting frequency and reporting mechanisms	☐
4. Member Engagement Strategy	Define who can join (open to all, specific groups)	☐
	Create communication plan (email, Slack, intranet, etc.)	☐
	Design member onboarding and welcome plan	☐
5. Events & Initiatives Planning	Plan launch event or kick-off session	☐
	Identify 2–3 key initiatives for the first 6 months	☐

Stage	Action Item	Status
	Align events with business goals and cultural calendar	☐
6. Budget & Resources	Secure annual or quarterly ERG budget	☐
	Request access to internal tools, rooms, or platforms	☐
7. Metrics & Success Tracking	Define KPIs (participation, impact, engagement)	☐
	Set up tracking process (survey, dashboard, reports)	☐
8. Communication & Visibility	Announce ERG launch company-wide	☐
	Highlight in leadership updates, newsletters, or town halls	☐
	Create branding assets (logo, tagline, templates)	☐
9. Collaboration & Growth	Build relationships with other ERGs or external partners	☐
	Join ERG councils, forums, or DEI committees	☐
	Plan for leadership development and succession	☐

ERG Launch Checklist

1 Define Purpose & Scope
- ☐ Identify the business need or empbloyee interest for the ERG
- ☐ Define ERG mission, vision, and goals
- ☐ Align with company DEI or culture strategy

2 Executive Sponsorship
- ☐ Secure an executive sponsoor or leadership champion
- ☐ Define the sponsor's role and involvement expectations

3 Governance Structure
- ☐ Establish ERG leadershipe roles (Chair, Co-Chair, etc.)
- ☐ Create a charter or guiding document
- ☐ Decide on meeting frequency and reporting mechanisms

4 Member Engagement Strategy
- ☐ Define who can join (open to all, speccific groups)
- ☐ Create communication plan (email, Slack, intranet, etc.)
- ☐ Design member onboarding and welcome plan

5 Budget & Initiatives Planning
- ☐ Plan launch event or kick-off session
- ☐ Identify 2–3 key initiatives for the first t 6 months
- ☐ Align events with business goals and cultural calendar

6 Metrics & Success Tracking
- ☐ Define KPIs (participation, impact, engagemment)
- ☐ Set up tracking process (survey, dashboard, rereports)

8 Communication & Visibility
- ☐ Build relationships with other ERGs or eexternal partners
- ☐ Join ERG councils, forums, or DEI committees
- ☐ Plan for leadership development and succession

Case Study: How UnityCircle Transformed Employee Resource Groups with Innovative Solutions

Employee Resource Groups (ERGs) have long been recognized as a vital part of fostering diversity, inclusion, and employee engagement in organizations. However, building and maintaining effective ERGs can be challenging, especially as companies scale and their diversity initiatives evolve. In this **ERG case study**, we dive into how **UnityCircle** has helped organizations transform their ERG programs into thriving communities of support, leadership, and innovation.

Background: The Challenge of Scaling ERGs

For many companies, ERGs represent a critical step towards achieving Diversity, Equity, and Inclusion (DEI) goals. However, scaling ERGs to have a measurable impact requires careful planning, consistent engagement, and the right tools to streamline operations and track success.

Before leveraging **UnityCircle**, many organizations struggled with:

- **Lack of visibility and engagement metrics**: It was difficult to track the performance and effectiveness of each ERG group.
- **Manual processes**: Managing ERG activities, events, and member engagement often involved a lot of time-consuming, manual effort.
- **Disconnected efforts**: There was often little coordination between different ERGs or alignment with broader company-wide DEI initiatives.

These challenges hindered the ability of ERGs to reach their full potential and show measurable results to leadership.

The Solution: UnityCircle's ERG Management Platform

UnityCircle is a platform designed to streamline the management of ERGs, providing organizations with the tools they need to launch, manage, and scale their employee communities. By offering a centralized, easy-to-use platform for ERG leaders, UnityCircle empowers organizations to:

1. **Create and manage multiple ERGs**: From defining the purpose of each group to assigning leadership roles and tracking participation, UnityCircle offers full management support.
2. **Drive engagement and collaboration**: Through integrated event management tools, mentorship programs, and communication channels, UnityCircle fosters meaningful engagement within ERGs.
3. **Measure impact**: The platform provides robust analytics and reporting tools that allow companies to track participation, gather feedback, and align ERG activities with broader business goals.

Key Features:

- **Dashboard for Real-Time Analytics**: ERG leaders can track member engagement, event participation, and feedback to assess the effectiveness of their activities.
- **Member Directory & Networking**: Employees can find and connect with others who share their values and interests, fostering a sense of community.

- **Event Management & Calendar Sync**: Plan and host events, track RSVPs, and integrate with company calendars to ensure maximum participation.

Let's look at how **UnityCircle** helped one particular company, **TechInnovate**, enhance their ERG efforts and achieve tangible results.

The Problem:

TechInnovate had several ERGs, but they were struggling with visibility and engagement. Although employees were passionate about the groups, the company lacked an easy way to manage the different ERGs and track their outcomes. The company wanted to:

- Increase participation in ERG activities.
- Align ERG goals with DEI and business objectives.
- Show leadership the impact of ERGs on employee engagement and retention.

The Implementation:

TechInnovate decided to implement UnityCircle to streamline their ERG management process. The solution involved:

1. **Consolidating all ERGs into one platform**: UnityCircle allowed TechInnovate to manage all their ERGs in one place, ensuring that leadership had visibility into the goals and activities of each group.
2. **Setting clear goals and measuring impact**: Each ERG leader worked with their team to set measurable objectives for their group. UnityCircle's analytics tools helped track member participation, event attendance,

and feedback, making it easy to see how well each ERG was meeting its goals.
3. **Fostering cross-ERG collaboration**: UnityCircle's communication features helped break down silos between different ERGs, allowing them to collaborate on larger DEI initiatives and share best practices.

The Results:

After implementing UnityCircle, TechInnovate experienced several positive outcomes:

- **Increased engagement**: ERG participation rates grew by 30% within the first six months. Employees felt more connected to their communities and were more actively involved in events and initiatives.
- **Clearer alignment with DEI objectives**: ERG leaders were able to align their activities with TechInnovate's overarching DEI strategy, helping to drive more meaningful and impactful initiatives.
- **Improved retention and job satisfaction**: Feedback surveys showed that employees involved in ERGs felt more supported and connected to the company, leading to a noticeable improvement in retention and overall job satisfaction.

Conclusion: The Power of UnityCircle for ERGs

This **ERG case study** demonstrates the powerful impact that the right tools can have on scaling and optimizing ERG programs. With **UnityCircle**, organizations like TechInnovate can:

- Streamline ERG management
- Foster deeper engagement and collaboration

- Measure the success and impact of their ERGs on DEI outcomes

The **UnityCircle success story** highlights how a robust ERG platform can help organizations overcome the challenges of scaling ERGs and create lasting impact. By leveraging the right technology, companies can empower their employees, improve retention, and build a more inclusive, engaged workforce.

Ready to Take Your ERGs to the Next Level?

Are you ready to transform your ERG program? Download the **UnityCircle platform** today and discover how it can help you manage and scale your ERGs for maximum impact.

☐ **Request a Demo** to see UnityCircle in action and learn how our ERG platform can drive meaningful DEI outcomes at your organization.

Final Thoughts: ERGs are a powerful tool for fostering diversity, inclusion, and belonging within organizations. With the right platform like UnityCircle, ERGs can go beyond just being employee groups—they become a key driver of business success and culture transformation.

Why ERGs Matter in 2025

The Growing Importance of Employee Resource Groups in Modern Workplaces

In 2025, the workplace is not just about productivity—it's about **people, purpose, and belonging**. As hybrid work models, cultural transformation, and DEI (Diversity, Equity, and Inclusion) continue to shape organizational priorities, **Employee Resource Groups (ERGs)** have emerged as essential pillars of a healthy, high-performing workplace.

But why do ERGs matter now more than ever? Let's explore the **importance of ERGs** and the **benefits of ERGs** for employees and companies alike.

The Shift Toward Inclusive, Connected Workplaces

The past few years have radically transformed how companies view employee engagement. The rise of Gen Z in the workforce, the call for social responsibility, and the need for inclusive leadership have made it clear: **companies can't afford to ignore community and culture**.

ERGs meet this moment perfectly. They give employees a voice, create space for identity and belonging, and align deeply with the values of modern organizations.

1. ERGs Build Belonging in a Fragmented World

In an era of remote and hybrid work, employees are more **physically disconnected** than ever. ERGs act as virtual campfires—places where employees can gather around shared experiences, cultures, and goals.

Belonging isn't just a feeling—it's a key driver of performance, loyalty, and innovation.

By fostering genuine connections, ERGs help reduce isolation and improve employee morale.

2. ERGs Drive Real Business Value

The **benefits of ERGs** extend far beyond social connection. Leading companies report that active ERGs lead to:

- Higher retention rates
- Increased employee engagement
- Faster internal mobility
- More diverse leadership pipelines

According to McKinsey, organizations in the top quartile for ethnic and gender diversity outperform their peers financially. ERGs are one of the most effective internal levers to activate that diversity.

3. ERGs Are Strategic DEI Engines

DEI goals are no longer confined to HR—they're board-level priorities. ERGs provide **on-the-ground insight** into employee needs, helping organizations:

- Identify policy gaps
- Test inclusive practices
- Launch company-wide initiatives
- Hold leadership accountable

In 2025, ERGs are seen not as side projects, but as **embedded DEI infrastructure** that drive measurable outcomes.

4. ERGs Foster Leadership Development

ERGs offer an incredible sandbox for **emerging leaders**. Employees who serve as ERG leads often:

- Gain cross-functional visibility
- Learn budgeting, project management, and communication
- Influence company-wide decisions

Companies that invest in ERGs are also **investing in their future leadership**—especially leaders from underrepresented groups.

5. ERGs Align People with Purpose

Employees want to work for companies that reflect their values. ERGs help build that alignment by:

- Creating channels for advocacy
- Supporting community impact efforts
- Elevating cultural observances and identity-based events

In 2025, a strong ERG program signals to candidates and customers that your company **walks the talk** when it comes to inclusion.

The Importance of ERGs in a Competitive Talent Market

In a talent-driven economy, culture is your competitive edge. **Companies with active, well-supported ERGs are**

more attractive to top talent, especially those from Gen Z and diverse backgrounds.

Employees today want more than compensation—they want community, purpose, and a sense of belonging. That's exactly what ERGs deliver.

UnityCircle: Empowering the Future of ERGs

At **UnityCircle**, we're building the operating system for modern ERGs. Our platform empowers companies to:

- Launch and scale ERGs easily
- Provide structure, funding, and governance
- Track participation, impact, and engagement
- Support ERG leaders with training and resources

We believe ERGs are not a trend—they're the future of work.

Final Thoughts

The **importance of ERGs** in 2025 is undeniable. From driving culture and engagement to delivering business impact, ERGs are now a core part of organizational success. Companies that invest in them aren't just doing the right thing—they're doing the smart thing.

Ready to unlock the power of ERGs in your organization?
☐ Schedule a demo with UnityCircle and start building community that matters.

Indian Companies with Active ERGs

Several leading companies in India have embraced Employee Resource Groups (ERGs) to foster diversity, equity, inclusion, and belonging. These ERGs support various communities, including women, LGBTQIA+ individuals, persons with disabilities, veterans, and others. Here are some notable examples:Akamai

---

1. Infosys

Infosys has established multiple ERGs to support its diverse workforce:

- **iWIN**: Infosys Women's Inclusivity Network for women employees and their allies.
- **InfyAbility**: Focused on employees with disabilities and their allies.
- **iPride**: Supports members of the LGBTQ+ community and their allies.
- **Family Matters**: Centers on parenting, relationships, health, and wellness.
- **Multicultural ERG (MERG)**: Celebrates a multicultural workforce and promotes cross-cultural collaboration.
- **InfyVets**: For military veterans and their allies.
- **iBELIEVE**: Supports Black employees and their allies.
  AIHR+6Infosys+6foundit india+6

2. Tata Consultancy Services (TCS)

TCS supports ERGs for women, LGBTQ+ employees, and other underrepresented groups. These ERGs provide platforms for employees to voice concerns, share experiences, and contribute to the company's DEI strategy. They also organize internal events and workshops to promote diversity awareness. foundit india+2Amazing Workplaces+2CoffeePals+2

3. Wipro

Wipro has developed significant programs to foster diversity and inclusion:

- **Wipro Achieve**: Facilitates employment and career growth for persons with disabilities.
- **Wipro PRIDE**: An ERG that creates a welcoming space for LGBTQIA+ employees. foundit india

4. Mahindra & Mahindra

Mahindra has introduced gender-neutral policies supporting LGBTQ+ employees, including equal benefits for same-sex partners and gender transition support. The company also runs awareness campaigns and supports LGBTQ+ employees through ERGs that provide advocacy and community building. Amazing Workplaces

5. Godrej Group

Godrej has established a dedicated diversity and inclusion council and initiatives like the "Godrej India Culture Lab," which fosters LGBTQIA+ inclusion and gender equality through events and dialogues. foundit india

6. Axis Bank

Axis Bank has shown a robust commitment to diversity and inclusion with initiatives like the 'GIG-A Opportunities platform' for flexible work and the "ComeAsYouAre" charter aimed at the LGBTQIA+

community. The bank has also established supportive infrastructure for employees with disabilities. <u>foundit india+1Infosys+1</u>

7. WeWork India

WeWork India has several ERGs:

- **Enabled by We**: Champions accessibility and inclusivity for the Persons with Disabilities (PWD) community.
- **Women of We**: Elevates women in the workplace through professional and personal growth opportunities.
- **Satrangi**: Creates a supportive environment for LGBTQIA+ employees and allies.
- **Tails of We**: Advocates for animal welfare. <u>Diversity Woman+2WeWork India+2Akamai+2</u>

8. Optum India

Optum India's ERGs provide team members opportunities to share their authentic selves and build connections. For instance, the **Women LEAD – India** ERG facilitates professional development for female colleagues and has hosted events featuring inspiring figures like Paralympian Deepa Malik. <u>LinkedIn</u>

9. Adobe India

Adobe has several ERGs active in India:

- **Access at Adobe**: Focuses on accessibility.
- **Pride at Adobe**: Supports LGBTQ+ employees.
- **Women at Adobe**: Empowers women in the workplace.
- **Veterans at Adobe**: Supports military veterans. <u>People Matters+1Diversity</u>

10. Dell India

Dell's ERGs are voluntary, employee-led communities that drive belonging and professional growth. They have 13 ERGs with more than 469 chapters worldwide, including:

- **Asians in Action**
- **Black Networking Alliance**
- **Conexus**
- **Family Balance**
- **GenNext**
- **Interfaith**
- **Latino Connection**

These examples illustrate the growing commitment of Indian companies to foster inclusive workplaces through ERGs. Such groups not only support underrepresented communities but also contribute to organizational growth by enhancing employee engagement and satisfaction.

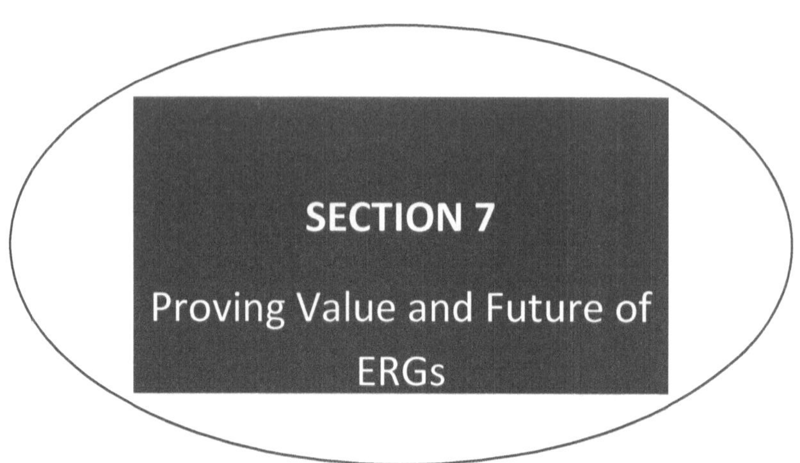

SECTION 7
Proving Value and Future of
ERGs

How to Measure ERG Success

The Key Metrics Every Company Should Track to Measure ERG Impact

Employee Resource Groups (ERGs) play a critical role in building inclusive workplaces, but their success is often difficult to quantify. As ERGs evolve from passion projects into strategic business drivers, companies must learn **how to measure ERG impact** effectively.

In this article, we'll explore the most valuable **ERG metrics** and provide a framework for understanding whether your ERGs are truly moving the needle.

Why ERG Metrics Matter

Measuring the impact of ERGs serves multiple purposes:

- Justifies continued funding and executive support
- Highlights areas for growth or restructuring
- Demonstrates value to the broader organization
- Helps ERG leaders make data-informed decisions

While culture is hard to measure, ERGs can and should be held to performance standards—just like any other business initiative.

The Four Dimensions of ERG Success

A well-rounded measurement strategy includes both **quantitative** and **qualitative** ERG metrics across four key dimensions:

1. Engagement Metrics

These show how many people are connecting with the ERG and how actively they're involved.

- Number of active members
- Event attendance and frequency
- Membership growth rate
- Participation across locations or departments
- Engagement on communication channels (Slack, email, forums)

Tip: Compare participation data against overall workforce demographics to identify reach and gaps.

---

2. Program and Event Effectiveness

Tracking event quality and relevance helps ensure ERG activities align with members' needs.

- Event satisfaction scores
- Post-event feedback and testimonials
- Repeat attendance rates
- Number of events aligned with ERG goals (e.g., career growth, cultural awareness)

Pro tip: Use short surveys after each event to capture value delivered.

---

3. Organizational Impact Metrics

These **measure ERG impact** on broader company goals and employee experience.

- Retention rates of ERG members vs. non-members
- Promotion rates among ERG leaders
- Employee engagement survey scores by ERG participation
- Contributions to business initiatives (e.g., inclusive hiring, product feedback)

Example: A Women's ERG might partner with HR to improve promotion equity, then track results year-over-year.

---

4. Leadership and Development Metrics

ERGs are often talent incubators. Capture leadership growth with:

- Number of ERG leaders taking on broader company roles
- Participation in formal leadership development programs
- Skills gained (event planning, public speaking, budgeting)
- Mentorship or sponsorship pairings created by the ERG

Recognizing and reporting these outcomes can strengthen the ERG's influence across the company.

Qualitative Success Indicators

Don't ignore the power of stories and sentiment. Ask:

- What testimonials are emerging from ERG members?

- Has the ERG influenced policy, culture, or product development?
- Are executives increasingly leaning on ERGs for insight?
- Are new employees citing ERGs as a reason they joined or stayed?

Combine these narratives with hard metrics for a well-rounded story of success.

Common Pitfalls to Avoid

When building an ERG metrics framework, avoid:

- Focusing only on vanity metrics (like event headcounts)
- Measuring only outputs, not outcomes
- Ignoring ERG leader feedback
- Setting KPIs without considering ERG capacity

Remember: ERG success should reflect **real impact**, not just activity.

UnityCircle: Measure What Matters

At **UnityCircle**, we understand that measuring ERG success is essential to scaling programs and earning leadership support. Our platform includes:

- Real-time ERG dashboards
- Participation and engagement tracking
- Custom KPIs tailored to your DEI strategy
- Impact reports that connect ERG activities to business outcomes

☐ **Ready to track and grow your ERG impact?** <u>Book a demo with UnityCircle</u> and start measuring what matters.

Final Thoughts

ERGs are powerful—but without clear measurement, their contributions can go unnoticed. By tracking the right **ERG metrics** and aligning them with your organizational goals, you can move from intention to influence.

When you know how to **measure ERG impact**, you don't just prove value—you improve it.

Proving the ROI of ERGs

How to Quantify the Value of ERGs to Your Organization

Employee Resource Groups (ERGs) have become essential for driving inclusion, engagement, and innovation in the workplace. But as companies continue to invest time, resources, and executive support into ERGs, a key question arises: **What's the return on investment?**

In this article, we break down how to evaluate **ERG ROI** and demonstrate the **value of ERGs** in a way that resonates with both HR and executive leadership.

Why ERG ROI Matters

While ERGs were once seen as volunteer-led passion projects, today they are strategic tools that:

- Strengthen employee engagement
- Improve retention and promotion equity
- Drive innovation through diverse perspectives
- Attract talent through inclusive culture

However, without clear metrics, ERGs risk being undervalued or underfunded. Proving **ERG ROI** helps validate the business case—and ensures long-term support.

Let's explore the different ways ERGs generate measurable and strategic value:

1. Talent Retention and Engagement

ERGs create belonging, which leads to loyalty. Studies show:

- Employees involved in ERGs are more likely to stay with a company
- ERG participation correlates with higher engagement scores
- ERG leadership roles boost internal mobility and promotions

ROI Metric Example:
Compare retention rates between ERG members vs. non-members over a 12-month period.

---

2. Leadership Development

Serving as an ERG leader develops skills in:

- Project and event management
- Budget oversight
- Cross-functional collaboration
- Public speaking and executive engagement

ROI Metric Example:
Track the career growth and promotions of ERG leaders compared to non-participating peers.

3. Recruiting and Employer Branding

Companies with visible ERG programs appeal to diverse candidates. ERGs:

- Participate in recruitment fairs and affinity conferences
- Contribute to inclusive onboarding experiences
- Enhance employer brand storytelling

ROI Metric Example:
Survey new hires to determine how ERGs influenced their decision to join the company.

4. Innovation and Product Impact

ERGs often provide insights that lead to better products and services. For example:

- LGBTQ+ ERGs consulting on inclusive advertising
- Disability ERGs advising on accessibility improvements
- Multicultural ERGs helping localize content or UX

ROI Metric Example:
Track the number of product or policy changes influenced by ERG feedback.

---

5. Crisis Response and Cultural Insight

During social or global events, ERGs provide timely input and guidance that helps organizations respond authentically and internally support impacted employees.

ROI Metric Example:
Document and share case studies where ERG involvement shaped internal communications or public statements.

How to Calculate ERG ROI

Here's a simple formula to conceptualize:

ERG ROI = (Tangible + Intangible Value Created) / Resources Invested

Break it down into:

- **Tangible value**: reduced turnover costs, faster leadership development, increased employee referrals
- **Intangible value**: improved culture, DEI brand equity, internal trust and morale
- **Investment**: ERG budgets, time, software, training, and executive support

To resonate with business leaders:

- **Speak in metrics**: Link ERGs to KPIs like retention, engagement, and innovation
- **Share testimonials**: Combine data with real stories of impact
- **Create dashboards**: Visualize ERG activity and outcomes over time
- **Benchmark performance**: Compare to other companies or previous years

---

ERG Value Metrics

1. **ERG Membership Growth**
   - Number of members over time (by ERG, location, department, etc.)
   - Growth rate (%) month-over-month or quarter-over-quarter
2. **Event Participation**
   - Attendance rates (number & percentage of invitees)
   - Repeat participation rate (returning attendees)
   - No-show/dropout rate
3. **Active Participation**
   - % of members engaging in activities (vs passive members)
   - Number of posts/comments/interactions in ERG forums or chats

Operational Metrics

4. **Number of Events and Activities Organized**
   o By ERG group and type (social, professional, volunteering)
5. **Budget Utilization**
   o Funds allocated vs. funds used
   o Cost per participant/event
6. **Time Invested**
   o Volunteer hours contributed by ERG leaders and members
7. **Cross-functional Involvement**
   o ERG activities involving multiple business units or teams

Strategic Impact Metrics

8. **Retention Rates of ERG Members vs. Non-members**
   o Higher retention may indicate ERG's positive impact
9. **Promotion & Advancement Rates**
   o Comparing members vs. non-members, especially for underrepresented groups
10. **Talent Acquisition Support**

- Number of referrals from ERG members
- ERG-influenced hires (e.g., from outreach events)

11. **Employee Engagement Scores (Pre/Post Involvement)**

- Based on pulse surveys or company-wide engagement tools

12. **Qualitative Feedback from Members**

- Open-ended survey responses
- Thematic analysis from forums and post-event feedback

13. **Belonging Index / Inclusion Sentiment Score**

- Self-reported sense of belonging pre/post joining an ERG

14. **Net Promoter Score (NPS) for ERGs**

- "How likely are you to recommend this ERG to a colleague?"

15. **Number of ERG Leaders Developed**

- People who took on leadership roles within ERGs
- Leadership skill development through ERG participation

16. **ERG Leader Turnover Rate**

- Stability and continuity of ERG leadership

17. **Executive Sponsorship Engagement**

- Number of interactions by executive sponsors
- Sponsor attendance at events

Collaboration & Impact Metrics

18. Inter-ERG Collaborations

- Joint events or initiatives across multiple ERGs

19. Community or External Partnerships

- Number and impact of community outreach programs

20. Business Unit Collaboration

- Initiatives that involve other departments (e.g., HR, L&D, Marketing)

Bonus: Dashboards to Visualize Metrics

You could categorize metrics into dashboards such as:

- **Engagement & Participation**
- **Leadership & Impact**
- **Diversity & Inclusion Outcomes**
- **ROI & Budget Use**

UnityCircle: Built to Showcase ERG ROI

At **UnityCircle**, we understand the challenge of proving ERG value. That's why our platform includes:

- Dashboards for tracking ERG engagement and influence
- KPI templates aligned to DEI and business outcomes

* Reporting tools to help ERG leaders tell their impact story

☐ **Want to make your ERGs unignorable?** <u>Book a demo with UnityCircle</u> and start proving ROI with confidence.

Final Thoughts

ERGs are no longer a "nice to have." They are **strategic assets**—but only if their impact is seen and supported. By tracking and communicating **ERG ROI**, organizations can elevate these groups from the margins to the core of culture and growth.

The future of work is inclusive—and the numbers prove it.

Using Data to Improve ERG Performance

How ERG Analytics and Dashboards Can Drive Smarter, More Impactful Resource Groups

Employee Resource Groups (ERGs) are a powerful engine for inclusion, engagement, and innovation within modern workplaces. But like any business initiative, their effectiveness depends on more than just enthusiasm—it requires insight. With the right **ERG analytics** and **ERG dashboards**, companies can unlock new levels of performance and impact.

In this article, we explore how organizations can leverage data to guide decisions, improve ERG programs, and drive measurable outcomes.

Why Data Matters for ERGs

Historically, many ERGs have operated informally, without consistent tracking of goals, membership, or outcomes. This lack of data can limit visibility, reduce executive support, and make it hard to scale successful programs.

By embracing **ERG analytics**, organizations can:

- Align ERG efforts with company-wide goals
- Identify what's working—and what isn't
- Empower ERG leaders with actionable insights
- Justify funding and strategic investment

What to Measure: Key ERG Performance Metrics

To build an effective analytics strategy, start by tracking metrics across four core areas:

1. Membership & Engagement

- Total number of active members
- Growth rate over time
- Participation in events, programs, or discussions
- New vs. returning attendees

Use case: If engagement drops, ERG leaders can adapt content or outreach methods.

2. Event Performance

- Event attendance and no-show rates
- Post-event feedback/surveys
- Event costs vs. perceived value
- Repeat participation metrics

Use case: Identify which formats (e.g., workshops vs. panels) resonate best with your audience.

---

3. Leadership Development

- Number of ERG leaders promoted internally
- Involvement in leadership programs or mentorship
- Skills developed through ERG roles (tracked via self-assessment or 360 reviews)

Use case: Use ERG leadership as a pipeline for DEI and business leadership roles.

---

4. Business and Cultural Impact

- Correlation between ERG participation and retention
- Policy or product changes driven by ERG insights
- Improvement in employee engagement scores among ERG participants

Use case: Showcase how ERGs contribute to tangible culture and business outcomes.

The Power of ERG Dashboards

ERG dashboards transform raw data into visual insights. A well-designed dashboard enables ERG leaders, HR partners, and executives to:

- Monitor key performance indicators (KPIs)
- Compare ERG activity across teams or locations
- Spot engagement trends and gaps
- Generate reports for stakeholders in seconds

Pro tip: Use role-based access so ERG leaders see day-to-day insights, while executives get a high-level strategic view.

Best Practices for ERG Data and Analytics

Set Clear Goals Early

Define success upfront. Are you trying to increase participation, reduce turnover, or drive innovation? Metrics should align with those outcomes.

Automate Data Collection

Where possible, integrate your ERG platform with HR systems, email, and calendar tools to reduce manual tracking.

Combine Quantitative + Qualitative

Pair numbers with stories. Survey comments, testimonials, and success stories add meaning to metrics.

Share Insights Regularly

Build a cadence for reviewing dashboards with ERG leads
and executive sponsors—quarterly, at minimum.

Adapt Based on Findings

Let your analytics drive decision-making. If something's
not working, the data will tell you.

UnityCircle: Your ERG Analytics Hub

At **UnityCircle**, we help companies measure and scale
what matters. Our all-in-one platform provides:

- Custom **ERG dashboards** for each group and region
- Automatic tracking of engagement, leadership, and
  impact metrics
- Survey tools for gathering feedback
- Benchmarking reports to compare across industries

Want to use data to power your ERG growth? Book a
demo with UnityCircle and see how analytics can unlock
your ERG potential.

Final Thoughts

In today's data-driven world, ERGs can no longer run on
instinct alone. By embracing **ERG analytics** and real-
time dashboards, organizations can elevate their programs
from good intentions to strategic drivers of inclusion and
innovation.

Because what gets measured—gets improved.

The Integral Role of ERGs in DEI

These employee-led groups not only foster a sense of belonging but also drive tangible outcomes that align with business objectives.

ERGs are voluntary, employee-led groups that bring together individuals with shared identities or interests, such as race, gender, or sexual orientation. Their primary goal is to create a supportive environment that promotes inclusivity and addresses the unique challenges faced by their members.LinkedIn

According to a McKinsey & Company article, effective ERGs align their initiatives with both corporate and employee expectations, thereby enhancing the overall inclusivity of the workplace. McKinsey & Company

---

Enhancing Recruitment and Retention

ERGs play a significant role in attracting and retaining diverse talent. By showcasing an organization's commitment to DEI, ERGs can influence potential candidates' perceptions and decisions. For instance, Hinge Health reported that 15% to 20% of new employees cited the company's DEI webpage, highlighting ERG initiatives, as a factor in their decision to join. Diversity ResourcesCulture Amp

Moreover, ERGs provide a platform for underrepresented employees to voice their concerns and contribute to organizational change, leading to increased job satisfaction and reduced turnover.

Driving Inclusive Workplace Practices

ERGs contribute to creating an inclusive workplace by:

- **Providing Safe Spaces**: They offer environments where employees can share experiences and challenges without fear of judgment. Wikipedia+2LinkedIn+2HRMorning+2
- **Influencing Policy and Culture**: ERGs can advocate for policy changes and cultural shifts that promote inclusivity.
- **Facilitating Professional Development**: Through workshops and mentorship programs, ERGs support the career growth of their members.

A study by Culture Amp emphasizes that ERGs empower employees to drive meaningful impact across various organizational areas. Culture Amp

Strategic Alignment with Business Goals

For ERGs to be effective, they must align their activities with the organization's strategic objectives. This includes: WIRED+3The Diversity Movement+3Vogue Business+3

- **Collaborating with Leadership**: Engaging with executives to ensure ERG initiatives support broader business goals.
- **Measuring Impact**: Utilizing metrics to assess the effectiveness of ERG programs and their contribution to DEI outcomes.

- **Securing Resources**: Advocating for necessary funding and support to sustain ERG activities.<u>The Diversity Movement</u>

The Diversity Movement highlights the importance of executive sponsorship in amplifying ERG efforts and ensuring their integration into the company's strategic framework. <u>The Diversity Movement</u>

Conclusion

ERGs are instrumental in driving DEI outcomes by fostering inclusive workplace environments, enhancing talent acquisition and retention, and aligning with organizational goals. By leveraging the unique insights and experiences of their members, ERGs not only support underrepresented groups but also contribute to the overall success and innovation of the organization.

Measuring the Impact of ERGs on Retention

To prove the link between **ERGs and retention**, companies should track:

- Retention rates of ERG members vs. non-members
- ERG membership growth over time
- Feedback from exit interviews about inclusion and support
- Engagement surveys broken down by ERG participation

These data points help quantify ERG value and inform future strategy.

UnityCircle: Empowering Retention Through ERGs

At **UnityCircle**, we understand how vital ERGs are to employee satisfaction and long-term loyalty. Our platform is built to support retention by:

- Providing engagement dashboards for ERG activity
- Enabling recognition and development for ERG leaders
- Offering surveys and feedback tools to track sentiment
- Helping HR teams visualize impact and align ERGs with business goals

Want to boost retention through inclusion? Schedule a demo with UnityCircle and see how ERGs can reduce churn and increase belonging.

Final Thoughts

ERGs are no longer just a DEI initiative—they are **strategic retention tools** that build culture, loyalty, and leadership from within. In a workplace where people want more than just a paycheck, ERGs give them purpose, connection, and a reason to stay.

If you're serious about keeping your best people, invest in the structures that help them thrive.

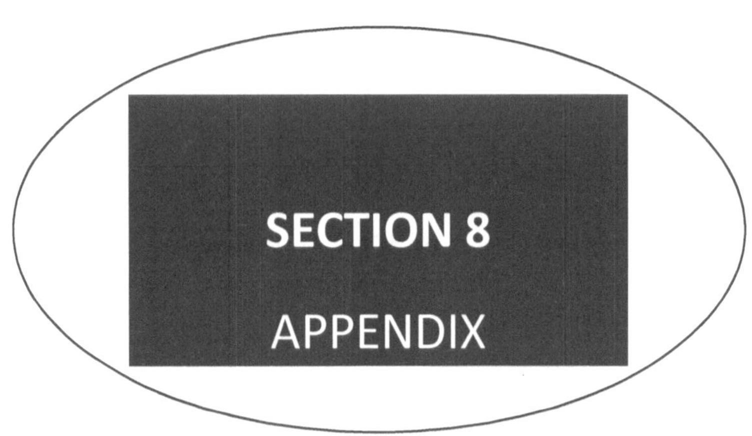

SECTION 8

APPENDIX

About the author

Santhana Selvan – Community Leader | Strategist | ERG Coach | Author

Santhana Selvan is a seasoned community leader with 25 years of experience in the IT industry and a deep passion for building inclusive, purpose-driven communities. As the **Bicycle Mayor of Hyderabad**, he leads a 10,000-member cycling movement, fostering sustainable mobility and active citizenship. With over 7 years of leadership in **Employee Resource Groups (ERGs)** at Reckitt, he specializes in creating grassroots workplace communities that boost belonging, wellbeing, and productivity.

Santhana is the founder of **UnityCircle**, a platform empowering companies to activate, manage, and scale ERGs for measurable impact. As a **Community Strategist and ERG Consultant**, he partners with organizations to design ERG governance, motivate employee participation, and embed diversity and inclusion at the core of culture.

He believes that **"great workplaces are built on great communities"** and envisions a future where connection, collaboration, and community drive personal and organizational success.

About the book

Discover the Hidden Engine of Workplace Transformation

In today's fast-paced, disconnected corporate world, employees crave more than just a paycheck—they seek purpose, belonging, and joy. **Employee Resource Groups (ERGs)** and micro-communities offer the formal-informal structure companies need to unlock human potential, drive innovation, and build truly inclusive cultures.

In *The Hidden Powerful Force at Work*, **Santhana Selvan—community strategist, ERG coach, and workplace happiness advocate—lays out a practical and visionary roadmap** to creating thriving micro-communities inside organizations of any size. From emotional architecture to scientific evidence, launch checklists to business impact dashboards, this book offers both inspiration and implementation.

Whether you're an HR leader, DEI champion, startup founder, ERG lead, or simply an employee seeking connection, this book will equip you to:

- Build ERGs that go beyond events to drive real culture change
- Improve retention, inclusion, and innovation through communities
- Measure the ROI of belonging with actionable metrics
- Design workplaces where every person feels seen, valued, and empowered

Because when employees lead communities, companies lead industries.